C# Design Pattern

Essentials

Tony Bevis

Ability First Limited
Essex, United Kingdom

C# Design Pattern Essentials

British Library Cataloguing in Publication Data. A catalogue record for this book is available from the British Library.

Publishing history:

- First edition, November 2012

Published by:

Ability First Limited

Dragon Enterprise Centre, 28 Stephenson Road

Leigh-on-Sea, Essex SS9 5LY, United Kingdom

www.abilityfirst.co.uk/books

ISBN: 978-0-9565758-6-9

Cover image by Ivan Polushkin, copyright Fotolia.

C# Design Pattern

Essentials

This book is dedicated to

"The Gang of Four"

Table of Contents

Preface

This book is an introductory guide to the world of object-oriented software design patterns. The examples and code extracts have been deliberately kept simple, allowing you to concentrate on understanding the concepts and application of each pattern rather than having to wade through irrelevant source code.

The book assumes that you have at least a basic knowledge of the C# programming language, including understanding what is meant by the terms encapsulation, inheritance and polymorphism, and that you know how to write classes and interfaces. By the end of this book you should be able to apply that knowledge to the design of complex applications, where objects from multiple classes need to interact to accomplish particular goals.

The patterns described within comprise all 23 of the patterns in the seminal work of Erich Gamma, Richard Helm, Ralph Johnson and John Vlissides; *Design Patterns: Elements of Reusable Object-Oriented Software* (Addison-Wesley, 1995). There are also four additional patterns described including Model-View-Controller (MVC), now a mainstay of graphical applications. For the most part, each chapter is self-contained, and you can therefore dip into the patterns in any order. However, it is recommended that you read Chapter 1 *"What are Design Patterns?"* first to familiarise yourself with the common theme and the object-oriented principles that the patterns utilise.

This book also makes use of a simplified implementation of Unified Modeling Language (UML) diagrams to show how the classes that comprise a pattern are structured. If you are unfamiliar with UML diagrams then you may wish to refer to Appendix A before you begin.

Prerequisite knowledge

In order to make use of this book you should have a basic understanding of both the C# language and of object-oriented principles. In particular, you should know how to create classes, interfaces and enums, and understand the terms encapsulation, inheritance, composition and polymorphism.

How this book is organised

Part I introduces the idea of design patterns, and lays the foundation for some simple core classes that comprise the common theme used throughout this book.

Part II describes the five creational patterns, that is, those that help manage the instantiation of objects.

Part III describes the seven structural patterns, that is, those that help manage how classes are organised and interrelate.

Part IV describes the eleven behavioural patterns, that is, those that help manage what the classes actually do.

Part V describes four additional patterns you should find useful in practical applications.

Part VI contains a single chapter that develops a simple 3-tier application that uses some of the more commonly used design patterns.

Part VII contains the appendixes, which includes a brief explanation of the Unified Modeling Language (UML) diagram formats for those unfamiliar with UML, and a quick reference for each of the 23 main patterns.

Conventions used in this book

C# code that you need to enter, or results that are shown as output, is shown in a fixed-width font as follows:

```
anObject.DoSomething();
anotherObject.DoThis();
```

Often, a piece of additional or modified code is provided, and those parts that are new or changed are indicated in **bold**:

```
anObject.DoSomethingElseInstead();
anObject.AlsoDoThis();
anotherObject.DoThis();
```

Names of classes, objects or C# statements will appear in the text using a fixed-width font such as `MyClass` or `someObject`, for example.

Where some useful or important additional information about a topic is included it will be shown in a note-box, like the following:

> This is some additional information in a note-box.

For reasons of brevity, `using` and `namespace` statements are omitted from most of the code samples in this book.

The book's resources

You can also download all of the C# source code from this book from our website:

```
http://www.abilityfirst.co.uk/books
```

Note to readers

This book is an adaptation of *Java Design Pattern Essentials – Second Edition* by the same author. It is possible that some of the text and code samples may reflect this adaptation in terms of the style and terminology differences between the languages. Readers' feedback is more than welcome.

Part I. Introduction

This part introduces the idea of design patterns, and lays the foundation for some simple core classes that comprise the common theme used throughout this book.

1.   What are Design Patterns?

Imagine that you have just been assigned the task of designing a software system. Your customer tells you that he needs to model the Gadgets his factory makes and that each Gadget comprises the same component parts but those parts are a bit different for each type of Gadget. And he also makes Gizmos, where each Gizmo comes with a selection of optional extras any combination of which can be chosen. And he also needs a unique sequential serial number stamped on each item made.

Just how would you go about designing these classes?

The chances are that no matter what problem domain you are working in, somebody else has had to design a similar solution in the past. Not necessarily for Gadgets and Gizmos of course, but conceptually similar in terms of objectives and structure. In other words there's a good chance that a generic solution or approach already exists, and all you need to do is to apply that approach to solve your design conundrum.

This is what *Design Patterns* are for. They describe generic solutions to software design problems. Once versed in patterns, you might think to yourself "those Gadgets could be modelled using the *Abstract Factory* pattern, the Gizmos using the *Decorator* pattern, and the serial number generation using the *Singleton* pattern."

How this book uses patterns

This book gives worked examples for each of the 23 patterns described in the classic reference work *Design Patterns – Elements of Reusable Object-Oriented Software* (Gamma, 1995) plus four additional useful patterns, including Model-View-Controller (MVC).

Each of the worked examples in this book uses a common theme drawn from the business world, being that of a fictional vehicle manufacturer called the Foobar Motor Company. The company makes a range of cars and vans together with the engines used to power the vehicles. You should therefore familiarise yourself with the classes described in this introduction.

The class hierarchy looks like this:

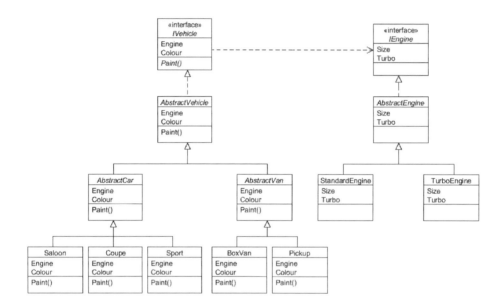

Figure 1.1 : IVehicle and IEngine class hierarchies

IVehicle and IEngine are the root interfaces of the hierarchies, with each vehicle object requiring a reference to an IEngine object. AbstractVehicle is an abstract class that implements the IVehicle interface, and AbstractEngine likewise implements the IEngine interface. For vehicles, we also have AbstractCar and AbstractVan together with concrete subclassses Saloon, Coupe and Sport as types of cars. AbstractVan has the concrete subclasses BoxVan and Pickup as types of van.

The concrete subclasses of AbstractEngine are StandardEngine and TurboEngine.

Despite there being several classes in the hierarchies the code for each has been kept deliberately simple so you can focus on understanding the patterns rather than having to decipher complex code. To illustrate this, here is the source code for the `IEngine` interface:

```
public interface IEngine
{
    int Size { get; }
    bool Turbo { get; }
}
```

This simple interface merely requires property getters to return the engine size (in cubic centimetres) and whether it is turbocharged.

The `AbstractEngine` class looks like this:

```
public abstract class AbstractEngine : IEngine
{
    private int size;
    private bool turbo;

    public AbstractEngine(int size, bool turbo)
    {
        this.size = size;
        this.turbo = turbo;
    }

    public virtual int Size
    {
        get
        {
            return size;
        }
    }

    public virtual bool Turbo
    {
        get
        {
            return turbo;
        }
    }

    public override string ToString()
    {
        return this.GetType().Name + " (" + size + ")";
    }
}
```

This simplified implementation of an engine requires the appropriate attributes to be supplied in the constructor. The `ToString()` method has been implemented to produce output in this format:

```
StandardEngine (1300)
TurboEngine (2000)
```

The `Equals()` and `GetHashCode()` methods will inherit from `object` and therefore use object identity. This makes sense, since for example, two separate 1300cc Standard Engines are logically different entities and so should be treated as such (one engine would go into one vehicle and the other engine into a different vehicle).

The concrete subclasses are trivially simple:

```
public class StandardEngine : AbstractEngine
{
    public StandardEngine(int size) : base(size, false)
    {
        // not turbocharged
    }
}


public class TurboEngine : AbstractEngine
{
    public TurboEngine(int size) : base(size, true)
    {
        // turbocharged
    }
}
```

Now that you have seen the `IEngine` hierarchy we can look at the `IVehicle` interface:

```
public interface IVehicle
{
    IEngine Engine { get; }
    VehicleColour Colour { get; }
    void Paint(VehicleColour colour);
}
```

A supporting enum called `VehicleColour` defines the possible colours that each `IVehicle` object could be:

```
public enum VehicleColour
{
    Unpainted, Blue, Black, Green,
    Red, Silver, White, Yellow
}
```

This is how the `AbstractVehicle` class implements `IVehicle`:

```
public abstract class AbstractVehicle : IVehicle
{
    private IEngine engine;
    private VehicleColour colour;

    public AbstractVehicle(IEngine engine)
        : this(engine, VehicleColour.Unpainted)
    {
    }

    public AbstractVehicle(IEngine engine, VehicleColour colour)
    {
        this.engine = engine;
        this.colour = colour;
    }

    public virtual IEngine Engine
    {
        get
        {
            return engine;
        }
    }

    public virtual VehicleColour Colour
    {
        get
        {
            return colour;
        }
    }

    public virtual void Paint(VehicleColour colour)
    {
        this.colour = colour;
    }

    public override string ToString()
    {
        return this.GetType().Name + " (" + engine + ", " +
                                            colour + ")";
    }
}
```

The overloaded constructors in `AbstractVehicle` require an `IEngine` object and optionally a vehicle colour to be supplied.

The output of calls to `ToString()` will be in this format:

```
Saloon (StandardEngine (1300), Red)
BoxVan (TurboEngine (2200), White)
```

The `AbstractCar` and `AbstractVan` classes just forward to the constructors (obviously real classes would define whatever is different between cars and vans):

```
public abstract class AbstractCar : AbstractVehicle
{
    public AbstractCar(IEngine engine)
        : this(engine, VehicleColour.Unpainted)
    {
    }

    public AbstractCar(IEngine engine, VehicleColour colour)
        : base(engine, colour)
    {
    }

}


public abstract class AbstractVan : AbstractVehicle
{
    public AbstractVan(IEngine engine)
        : this(engine, VehicleColour.Unpainted)
    {
    }

    public AbstractVan(IEngine engine, VehicleColour colour)
        : base(engine, colour)
    {
    }

}
```

The concrete subclasses also just forward to the constructors:

```
public class Saloon : AbstractCar
{
    public Saloon(IEngine engine)
```

```
                : this(engine, VehicleColour.Unpainted)
        {
        }

        public Saloon(IEngine engine, VehicleColour colour)
            : base(engine, colour)
        {
        }

}


public class Coupe : AbstractCar
{
    public Coupe(IEngine engine)
        : this(engine, VehicleColour.Unpainted)
    {
    }

    public Coupe(IEngine engine, VehicleColour colour)
        : base(engine, colour)
    {
    }

}


public class Sport : AbstractCar
{
    public Sport(IEngine engine)
        : this(engine, VehicleColour.Unpainted)
    {
    }

    public Sport(IEngine engine, VehicleColour colour)
        : base(engine, colour)
    {
    }

}


public class BoxVan : AbstractVan
{
    public BoxVan(IEngine engine)
        : this(engine, VehicleColour.Unpainted)
    {
    }

    public BoxVan(IEngine engine, VehicleColour colour)
        : base(engine, colour)
    {
    }

}
```

```
public class Pickup : AbstractVan
{
    public Pickup(IEngine engine)
        : this(engine, VehicleColour.Unpainted)
    {
    }

    public Pickup(IEngine engine, VehicleColour colour)
        : base(engine, colour)
    {
    }

}
```

Many of the patterns in this book utilise one or more of the above classes in some way, often adding additional functionality or classes for the purposes of explaining the pattern in question. You will also frequently see reference to a `Client` class; this just refers to whatever class is making use of the pattern under discussion.

How patterns are categorised

Each of the patterns described in this book fall under one of three categories; *Creational, Structural* or *Behavioural*:

- *Creational* patterns provide approaches to object instantiation. Where you place the `new` keyword affects how tightly or loosely coupled your classes are;

- *Structural* patterns provide approaches for combining classes and objects to form larger structures. Deciding whether to use inheritance or composition affects how flexible and adaptable your software is;

- *Behavioural* patterns provide approaches for handling communication between objects.

Common principles in design patterns

Experience has shown that some object-oriented approaches are more flexible than others. Here is a summary of the main principles that the patterns in this book strive to adhere to:

1. ***Program to an interface, not an implementation.*** By "interface" is meant the general concept of abstraction, which could refer to a C# interface or an abstract class. To accomplish this, use the most general type (e.g. interface) possible when declaring variables, constructor and method arguments, etc. Doing so gives extra flexibility as to the actual types that are used at run-time.

2. ***Prefer object composition over inheritance.*** Where a class is related to another in some way, you should distinguish between "is a" (or "is a type of") and "has a" relationships. In the `IVehicle` and `IEngine` hierarchies described earlier, it is true to say that `AbstractCar` "is a" `IVehicle`, and that `Saloon` "is a" `AbstractCar`. But it would not be true to say that `IVehicle` "is a" `IEngine`, but rather that an `IVehicle` "has a" `IEngine`. Therefore, inheritance is legitimately used for `AbstractCar` and `Saloon`, but object composition is used between `IVehicle` and `IEngine`. Do not be tempted to use inheritance just to save having to write some methods. Sometimes using a "has a" relationship is more flexible even when an "is a" relationship seems the natural choice. You will see an example of this in the *Decorator* pattern.

3. ***Keep objects loosely-coupled.*** Ideally, classes should model just one thing, and only be composed of other objects that are genuinely required (such as an `IVehicle` requiring an `IEngine`). Ask yourself what would happen if you wanted to use a class you have written in a completely different application; what "baggage" (i.e. other classes) would also need to be copied? By keeping this to a minimum, you make your class more re-usable. A good example of a pattern that uses loose-coupling is *Observer*.

4. ***Encapsulate the concept that varies.*** If you've written a class in which some parts are the same for each instance but another part of the class varies for each instance, consider extracting the latter into a class of its own, which is referenced by the original class. An example pattern that uses this principle is *Strategy*.

Some general advice

The principles listed above will become more apparent as we explore the patterns in detail. You should also note that the patterns described in this book give a general approach to a particular problem. It is quite acceptable for you to modify or adapt them to better fit your particular problem. And it is very common for multiple patterns to be combined to solve complex problems.

However, do remember that you should strive to keep things simple. It is easy, after reading a book such as this, to think that you have to find a pattern to solve a particular problem when an even simpler solution might be available. One of the mantras of Extreme Programming (XP) is "You aren't going to need it", the idea being that you should avoid adding features before they are required, and this philosophy could also be applied to patterns – beware of adding an unnecessary feature just so you can apply a pattern. Patterns are not a "magic bullet", just another set of tools in your toolkit, albeit an indispensable set.

Use your knowledge and experience to judge whether a pattern should be applied to your circumstances, and if so to what extent you need to adapt it. A good example of when applying patterns may be beneficial is when you are "refactoring" existing code. Refactoring is when you are changing the structure of some software but not its behaviour, to improve its maintainability and flexibility. This provides a good opportunity to examine your code to see if a pattern might provide a better structure, such as replacing conditionals, or defining factory classes to aid object instantiation.

Patterns have been applied to many programming languages besides C#, particularly object-oriented languages, and indeed other fields, having originated by being applied to architectural design. And new patterns are being developed and applied on a regular basis, so you may view this book as merely a starting point in the subject.

Part II. Creational Patterns

This part describes the five creational patterns, that is, those that help manage the instantiation of objects.

- *Abstract Factory*: Provide an interface for creating families of related or dependent objects without specifying their concrete classes;

- *Builder*: Separate the construction of a complex object from its representation so that the same construction process can create different representations;

- *Factory Method*: Define an interface for creating an object, but let subclasses decide which class to instantiate;

- *Prototype*: Specify the kinds of objects to create using a prototypical instance, and create new objects by copying the prototype;

- *Singleton*: Ensure a class allows only one object to be created, providing a single point of access to it.

2. Abstract Factory

Type	Creational
Purpose	Provide an interface for creating families of related or dependent objects without specifying their concrete classes.

The Foobar Motor Company makes cars and vans, which when being built comprises (among lots of other things) a body shell, a chassis and glassware for the windows. Although both cars and vans need all of the same types of components, the specifics of each type differ depending upon whether it is being used for a car or a van.

In other words:

- *A car's body shell is different from a van's body shell;*

- *A car's chassis is different from a van's chassis;*

- *A car's glassware is different from a van's glassware.*

Therefore, when we need to build a vehicle we can think of the components as coming from different 'families'; that is, when we build a car we use one family of components and when we build a van we use a different family of components.

We can thus model the components into simple hierarchies, as illustrated in the following figure:

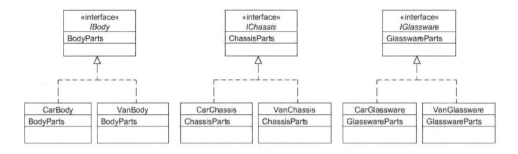

Figure 2.1 : IBody, IChassis & IGlassware class hierarchies

As you can see, there is an interface for `IBody` having implementations of `CarBody` and `VanBody`. Likewise we have similar separate hierarchies for `IChassis` and `IGlassware`.

The code for the `IBody` hierarchy is very simple:

```
public interface IBody
{
    string BodyParts { get; }
}

public class CarBody : IBody
{
    public virtual string BodyParts
    {
        get
        {
            return "Body shell parts for a car";
        }
    }
}

public class VanBody : IBody
{
    public virtual string BodyParts
    {
        get
        {
            return "Body shell parts for a van";
        }
    }
}
```

The code for the `IChassis` hierarchy is almost identical:

```csharp
public interface IChassis
{
    string ChassisParts { get; }
}

public class CarChassis : IChassis
{
    public virtual string ChassisParts
    {
        get
        {
            return "Chassis parts for a car";
        }
    }
}

public class VanChassis : IChassis
{
    public virtual string ChassisParts
    {
        get
        {
            return "Chassis parts for a van";
        }
    }
}
```

And likewise the code for the `IGlassware` hierarchy:

```csharp
public interface IGlassware
{
    string GlasswareParts { get; }
}

public class CarGlassware : IGlassware
{
    public virtual string GlasswareParts
    {
        get
        {
            return "Window glassware for a car";
        }
    }
}

public class VanGlassware : IGlassware
{
    public virtual string GlasswareParts
    {
```

```
        get
        {
            return "Window glassware for a van";
        }
    }
}
```

Now we need a way of getting the correct family of parts (either for a car or for a van) but without having to explicitly instantiate the specific type in client programs each time we require them. To accomplish this, we shall define "factory" classes that will do this for us:

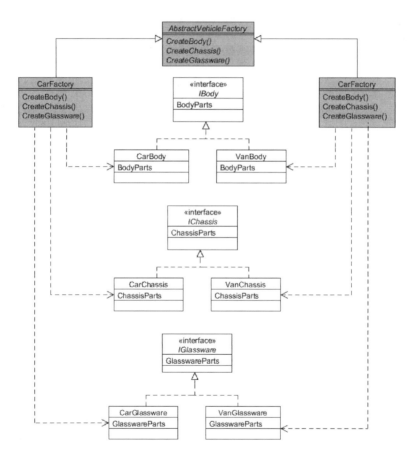

Figure 2.2 : Abstract Factory pattern

The `AbstractVehicleFactory` class is an abstract class that defines the abstract methods `CreateBody()`, `CreateChassis()` and

`CreateGlassware()`, **returning an** `IBody`, `IChassis` **and** `IGlassware`
object respectively:

```
public abstract class AbstractVehicleFactory
{
    public abstract IBody CreateBody();
    public abstract IChassis CreateChassis();
    public abstract IGlassware CreateGlassware();
}
```

The concrete subclass `CarFactory` **returns the objects specific for the car family:**

```
public class CarFactory : AbstractVehicleFactory
{
    public override IBody CreateBody()
    {
        return new CarBody();
    }

    public override IChassis CreateChassis()
    {
        return new CarChassis();
    }

    public override IGlassware CreateGlassware()
    {
        return new CarGlassware();
    }
}
```

The concrete subclass `VanFactory` **returns the objects specific for the van family:**

```
public class VanFactory : AbstractVehicleFactory
{
    public override IBody CreateBody()
    {
        return new VanBody();
    }

    public override IChassis CreateChassis()
    {
        return new VanChassis();
    }

    public override IGlassware CreateGlassware()
    {
        return new VanGlassware();
```

```
        }
    }
```

Now it just remains for client programs to instantiate the appropriate 'factory' after which it can obtain the correct parts without having to specify whether they are for a car or a van:

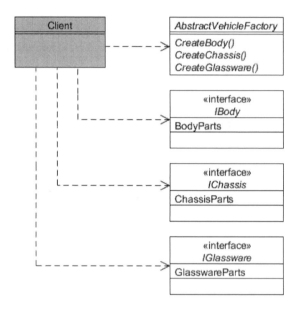

Figure 2.3 : How clients use Abstract Factory

```
string whatToMake = "car"; // or "van"

AbstractVehicleFactory factory = null;

// Create the correct 'factory'...
if (whatToMake.Equals("car"))
{
    factory = new CarFactory();
}
else
{
    factory = new VanFactory();
}

// Create the vehicle's component parts...
// These will either be all car parts or all van parts
IBody vehicleBody = factory.CreateBody();
```

```
IChassis vehicleChassis = factory.CreateChassis();
IGlassware vehicleGlassware = factory.CreateGlassware();

// Show what we've created...
Console.WriteLine(vehicleBody.BodyParts);
Console.WriteLine(vehicleChassis.ChassisParts);
Console.WriteLine(vehicleGlassware. GlasswareParts);
Console.Read();
```

Therefore your client program needs to know if it is making a car or a van, but once it has instantiated the correct factory all the methods to create the parts can be done using an identical set of method calls.

The main disadvantage of the *Abstract Factory* pattern arises if you need to add additional 'products'. For example, if we now need to include lights in the family of components, we would need to amend `AbstractVehicleFactory`, `CarFactory` and `VanFactory`, in addition to creating a new `ILights` hierarchy (`CarLights` and `VanLights`).

3. Builder

Type	Creational
Purpose	Separate the construction of a complex object from its representation so that the same construction process can create different representations.

The Foobar Motor Company makes cars and vans, and the construction process of each differs in detail; for example, the body shell of a van comprises a cab area and a large reinforced storage area, whereas a saloon car comprises a passenger area and a luggage area (i.e. boot). And of course there a number of complex steps that have to be undertaken regardless of what type of vehicle are being built.

The *Builder* pattern facilitates the construction of complex objects by separating the individual steps into separate methods in a *Builder* hierarchy, and then using a *Director* object to specify the required steps in the correct order. Finally, the finished product is retrieved from the *Builder*.

The following diagram shows these relationships:

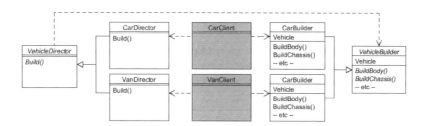

Figure 3.1 : Builder pattern

We start off with the abstract `VehicleBuilder` class:

```
public abstract class VehicleBuilder
{
    public virtual void BuildBody() {}
    public virtual void BuildBoot() {}
    public virtual void BuildChassis() {}
    public virtual void BuildPassengerArea() {}
    public virtual void BuildReinforcedStorageArea() {}
    public virtual void BuildWindows() {}

    public abstract IVehicle Vehicle {get;}
}
```

Note how this class defines all possible 'build' methods for both cars and vans, and provides empty implementations for each as a default. The abstract Vehicle property getter is for returning the finished vehicle.

The CarBuilder class inherits from VehicleBuilder and overrides the appropriate methods:

```
public class CarBuilder : VehicleBuilder
{
    private AbstractCar carInProgress;

    public CarBuilder(AbstractCar car)
    {
        carInProgress = car;
    }

    public override void BuildBody()
    {
        Console.WriteLine("building car body");
    }

    public override void BuildBoot()
    {
        Console.WriteLine("building car boot");
    }

    public override void BuildChassis()
    {
        Console.WriteLine("building car chassis");
    }

    public override void BuildPassengerArea()
    {
        Console.WriteLine("building car passenger area");
    }

    public override void BuildWindows()
    {
        Console.WriteLine("building car windows");
    }
```

```
    public override IVehicle Vehicle
    {
        get
        {
            return carInProgress;
        }
    }
}
```

Note that the `BuildReinforcedStorageArea()` method was not overridden since it is not applicable to cars.

The `VanBuilder` class overrides the appropriate methods to build a van:

```
public class VanBuilder : VehicleBuilder
{
    private AbstractVan vanInProgress;

    public VanBuilder(AbstractVan van)
    {
        vanInProgress = van;
    }


    public override void BuildBody()
    {
        Console.WriteLine("building van body");
    }

    public override void BuildChassis()
    {
        Console.WriteLine("building van chassis");
    }

    public override void BuildReinforcedStorageArea()
    {
        Console.WriteLine("building van storage area");
    }

    public override void BuildWindows()
    {
        Console.WriteLine("building van windows");
    }

    public override IVehicle Vehicle
    {
        get
        {
            return vanInProgress;
```

```
            }
        }
    }
```

Note that the `BuildBoot()` and `BuildPassengerArea()` methods were not overridden since they are not applicable to vans.

The `VehicleDirector` abstract class requires a `VehicleBuilder` object passed to its `Build()` method for implementation by subclasses:

```
public abstract class VehicleDirector
{
    public abstract IVehicle Build(VehicleBuilder builder);
}
```

The `CarDirector` class inherits from `VehicleDirector` and provides the step-by-step process for building a car:

```
public class CarDirector : VehicleDirector {

    public override IVehicle Build(VehicleBuilder builder)
    {
        builder.BuildChassis();
        builder.BuildBody();
        builder.BuildPassengerArea();
        builder.BuildBoot();
        builder.BuildWindows();
        return builder.Vehicle;
    }
}
```

The `VanDirector` class provides the step-by-step process for building a van:

```
public class VanDirector : VehicleDirector
{
    public override IVehicle Build(VehicleBuilder builder)
    {
        builder.BuildChassis();
        builder.BuildBody();
        builder.BuildReinforcedStorageArea();
        builder.BuildWindows();
        return builder.Vehicle;
    }
```

```
}
```

As an example of how to use the above classes, let's assume we want to
build a `Saloon` car:

```
AbstractCar car = new Saloon(new StandardEngine(1300));
VehicleBuilder builder = new CarBuilder(car);
VehicleDirector director = new CarDirector();
IVehicle v = director.Build(builder);
Console.WriteLine(v);
Console.Read();
```

You can see the required *Builder* object is constructed and passed to the
required *Director* object, after which we invoke the method to build the
product and then retrieve the finished article. The output should show:

```
Building car chassis
Building car body
Building car passenger area
Building car boot
Building car windows
Saloon (StandardEngine (1300), Unpainted)
```

4.   Factory Method

Type	Creational
Purpose	Define an interface for creating an object, but let subclasses decide which class to instantiate.

You will recall from the introduction the following class hierarchy for the vehicles made by the Foobar Motor Company:

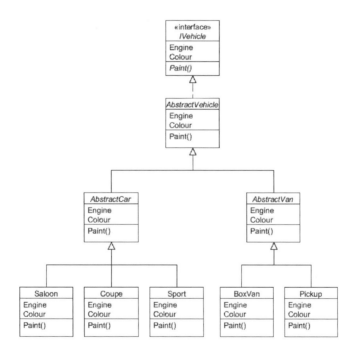

Figure 4.1 : IVehicle class hierarchy

When we need to instantiate a particular type of vehicle (such as a Coupe) it is often more flexible to define a separate class whose responsibility it is to manage the instantiation. This separate class is known as a *Factory*.

The *Factory Method* pattern defines an abstract class which serves as the 'factory' and that has an abstract method within to determine what product (in our case vehicle) to instantiate. Concrete subclasses of the factory make that determination. Here is how the *Factory Method* pattern could be used with the `IVehicle` class hierarchy:

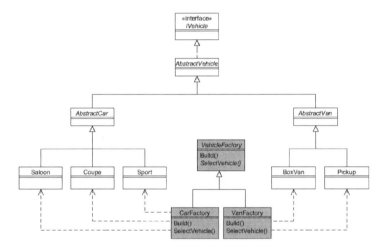

Figure 4.2 : Factory Method pattern

In the above diagram we can see that we have created an abstract `VehicleFactory` class which has two concrete subclasses, `CarFactory` and `VanFactory`. Let us look at how `VehicleFactory` is defined:

```
public abstract class VehicleFactory
{
    public enum DrivingStyle
    {
            Economical, Midrange, Powerful
    }

    public virtual IVehicle Build(DrivingStyle style,
                                  VehicleColour colour)
    {
        IVehicle v = SelectVehicle(style);
        v.Paint(colour);
        return v;
    }

    // This is the "factory method"
    protected internal abstract IVehicle SelectVehicle
                                        (DrivingStyle style);
```

}

VehicleFactory contains the public method Build() that takes as arguments the driving style (Economical, Midrange or Powerful[1]) and the colour that the vehicle should be painted. The Build() method calls the protected abstract SelectVehicle() method, which is the "factory method" after which the pattern is named. The implementation of SelectVehicle() is therefore delegated to the subclasses such that each subclass determines the specific type of vehicle to instantiate. The method is protected because we only want subclasses to utilise it – it is not intended to be invoked by clients.

Here is the CarFactory concrete subclass:

```
public class CarFactory : VehicleFactory
{
    protected internal override IVehicle SelectVehicle
                                        (DrivingStyle style)
    {
        if (style == DrivingStyle.Economical)
        {
            return new Saloon(new StandardEngine(1300));
        }
        else if (style == DrivingStyle.Midrange)
        {
            return new Coupe(new StandardEngine(1600));
        }
        else
        {
            return new Sport(new TurboEngine(2000));
        }
    }
}
```

As you can see, the SelectVehicle() method is implemented such that it works out from the supplied arguments exactly which type of car should be instantiated and returned.

The VanFactory is similar, using the argument to decide which van to instantiate and return:

```
public class VanFactory : VehicleFactory
```

---

[1]Defined as contants in the DrivingStyle enum.

```
    {
        protected internal override IVehicle SelectVehicle
                                            (DrivingStyle style)
        {
            if ((style == DrivingStyle.Economical) ||
                (style == DrivingStyle.Midrange))
            {
                return new Pickup(new StandardEngine(2200));
            }
            else
            {
                return new BoxVan(new TurboEngine(2500));
            }
        }
    }
}
```

Client programs instantiate the required factory and call its `Build()` method:

```
// I want an economical car, coloured blue...
VehicleFactory carFactory = new CarFactory();
IVehicle car = carFactory.Build(
                    VehicleFactory.DrivingStyle.Economical,
                    VehicleColour.Blue);
Console.WriteLine(car);

// I am a "white van man"...
VehicleFactory vanFactory = new VanFactory();
IVehicle van = vanFactory.Build(
                    VehicleFactory.DrivingStyle.Powerful,
                    VehicleColour.White);
Console.WriteLine(van);

Console.Read();
```

You should see the following output:

```
Saloon (StandardEngine (1300), Blue)
BoxVan (TurboEngine(2500), White)
```

Using 'static' factory methods

A common and useful variation is to define a `static` factory method. Let's assume we define the following additional `enum` in the `VehicleFactory` class:

```
public enum Category
```

```
{
    Car, Van
}
```

Now we can define the following static `Make()` method also in `VehicleFactory` **that works out which subclass to instantiate:**

```
public static IVehicle Make(Category cat,
                            DrivingStyle style,
                            VehicleColour colour)
{
    VehicleFactory factory;

    if (cat == Category.Car)
    {
        factory = new CarFactory();
    }
    else
    {
        factory = new VanFactory();
    }

    return factory.Build(style, colour);
}
```

Using the `static Make()` method is very straightforward:

```
// Create a red sports car...
IVehicle sporty = VehicleFactory.Make
                        (VehicleFactory.Category.Car,
                        VehicleFactory.DrivingStyle.Powerful,
                        VehicleColour.Red);
Console.WriteLine(sporty);
```

This should give the following output:

```
Sport (TurboEngine (2000), Red)
```

5. Prototype

Type	Creational
Purpose	Specify the kinds of objects to create using a prototypical instance, and create new objects by copying the prototype.

We shall assume in this chapter that instantiating car and van objects is a time-consuming process, and we therefore need to find a way of speeding up instantiation time whenever we need a new vehicle object.

Here is a reminder of the `Vehicle` class hierarchy:

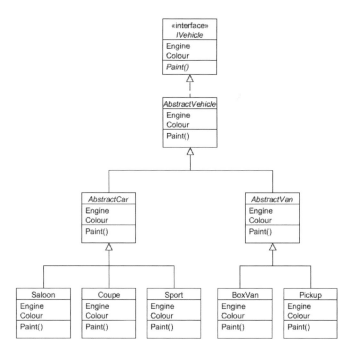

Figure 5.1 : IVehicle class hierarchy

One approach that may improve instantiation time is to utilise the C# cloning facilities. We will therefore specify that the IVehicle interface extends ICloneable and define the method Clone() inside AbstractVehicle. This chapter thus uses a modified version of the IVehicle interface and AbstractVehicle class as listed below, where the additional code is indicated in bold:

```csharp
public interface IVehicle : ICloneable
{
    IEngine Engine { get; }
    VehicleColour Colour { get; }
    void Paint(VehicleColour colour);
}


public abstract class AbstractVehicle : IVehicle
{
    private IEngine engine;
    private VehicleColour colour;

    public AbstractVehicle(IEngine engine)
            : this(engine, VehicleColour.UNPAINTED)
    {
    }

    public AbstractVehicle(IEngine engine, VehicleColour colour)
    {
        this.engine = engine;
        this.colour = colour;
        // ... followed by lots of time-consuming stuff
    }

    public virtual IEngine Engine
    {
        get
        {
            return engine;
        }
    }

    public virtual VehicleColour Colour
    {
        get
        {
            return colour;
        }
    }

    public virtual void Paint(VehicleColour colour)
    {
        this.colour = colour;
    }
```

```
    public virtual object Clone()
    {
        return this.MemberwiseClone();
    }

    public override string ToString()
    {
        return this.GetType().Name + " (" + engine + ", " +
                                        colour + ")";
    }
}
```

The `Clone()` method invokes the C# `MemberwiseClone()` method to perform the cloning of the receiving object.

None of the car or van subclasses needs to change since they inherit from `IVehicle` at the root of the hierarchy.

We will now define a `VehicleManager` class that will create the initial vehicles from which we can obtain clones:

```
public class VehicleManager
{
    private IVehicle saloon, coupe, sport, boxVan, pickup;

    public VehicleManager()
    {
        // For simplicity all vehicles use same engine type...
        saloon = new Saloon(new StandardEngine(1300));
        coupe = new Coupe(new StandardEngine(1300));
        sport = new Sport(new StandardEngine(1300));
        boxVan = new BoxVan(new StandardEngine(1300));
        pickup = new Pickup(new StandardEngine(1300));
    }

    public virtual IVehicle CreateSaloon()
    {
        return (IVehicle)saloon.Clone();
    }

    public virtual IVehicle CreateCoupe()
    {
        return (IVehicle)coupe.Clone();
    }

    public virtual IVehicle CreateSport()
    {
        return (IVehicle)sport.Clone();
    }

    public virtual IVehicle CreateBoxVan()
```

```
    {
        return (IVehicle)boxVan.Clone();
    }

    public virtual IVehicle CreatePickup()
    {
        return (IVehicle)pickup.Clone();
    }
```

Client programs can use VehicleManager as follows:

```
VehicleManager manager = new VehicleManager();

IVehicle saloon1 = manager.CreateSaloon();
IVehicle saloon2 = manager.CreateSaloon();
IVehicle pickup1 = manager.CreatePickup();

Console.WriteLine(saloon1);
Console.WriteLine(saloon2);
Console.WriteLine(pickup1);

Console.Read();
```

A drawback of VehicleManager as coded is that it always instantiates at least one vehicle of each type as part of the construction process. If not all types of vehicles will be needed, a more efficient technique would be to lazy-load by only instantiating the first time each is needed. This is illustrated in the modified version of the class (which we will call VehicleManagerLazy) below:

```
public class VehicleManagerLazy
{
    private IVehicle saloon, coupe, sport, boxVan, pickup;

    public VehicleManagerLazy()
    {
    }

    public virtual IVehicle CreateSaloon()
    {
        if (saloon == null)
        {
            saloon = new Saloon(new StandardEngine(1300));
        }
        return (IVehicle)saloon.Clone();
    }

    public virtual IVehicle CreateCoupe()
    {
```

```
        if (coupe == null)
        {
            coupe = new Coupe(new StandardEngine(1300));
        }
        return (IVehicle)coupe.Clone();
    }

    public virtual IVehicle CreateSport()
    {
        if (sport == null)
        {
            sport = new Sport(new StandardEngine(1300));
        }
        return (IVehicle)sport.Clone();
    }

    public virtual IVehicle CreateBoxVan()
    {
        if (boxVan == null)
        {
            boxVan = new BoxVan(new StandardEngine(1300));
        }
        return (IVehicle)boxVan.Clone();
    }

    public virtual IVehicle CreatePickup()
    {
        if (pickup == null)
        {
            pickup = new Pickup(new StandardEngine(1300));
        }
        return (IVehicle)pickup.Clone();
    }
}
```

Before a clone is returned, a check is made to ensure that the 'prototype' object exists, and it will be instantiated if necessary. From then on it just clones the previously instantiated object. Client programs can use VehicleManagerLazy in the same way as before:

```
VehicleManagerLazy manager = new VehicleManagerLazy();

IVehicle saloon1 = manager.CreateSaloon();
IVehicle saloon2 = manager.CreateSaloon();
IVehicle pickup1 = manager.CreatePickup();
```

6. Singleton

Type	Creational
Purpose	Ensure a class allows only one object to be created, providing a single point of access to it.

The Foobar Motor Company, in common with all vehicle manufacturers, needs to stamp a unique serial number on all vehicles they produce[1]. They want to model this requirement ensuring that there is just one easy place where the next available serial number can be obtained. If we were to have more than one object that generates the next number there is a risk that we could end up with separate numbering sequences, so we need to prevent this.

The *Singleton* pattern provides a way of ensuring that only one instance of a particular class can ever be created. So how can we stop other objects from just invoking `new` multiple times? There are several ways of accomplishing this, and the "traditional" approach that you may often encounter is to make your constructor `private` but provide a `public static` getter method that returns a `static` instance of the *Singleton* class. This is how it could look:

```
public class SerialNumberGenerator
{
    // static members
    private static volatile SerialNumberGenerator instance;

    public static SerialNumberGenerator Instance
    {
        get
        {
            if (instance == null)
            {
                instance = new SerialNumberGenerator();
            }
            return instance;
        }
    }
```

---

[1]In the UK this is known as the Vehicle Identification Number (VIN).

```
// instance variables
private int count;

// private constructor
private SerialNumberGenerator()
{
}

// instance methods
public virtual int NextSerial
{
    get
    {
        return ++count;
    }
}
}
}
```

Note that the `Instance` getter will only instantiate the object once and so the same instance will always be returned. The constructor is `private` to prevent client programs from calling `new`, thus enforcing the fact that only one object can ever be created, since they can only go through the `Instance` getter. The singleton could be used thus:

```
Console.WriteLine("next serial: " +
                    SerialNumberGenerator.Instance.NextSerial);

Console.WriteLine("next serial: " +
                    SerialNumberGenerator.Instance.NextSerial);

Console.WriteLine("next serial: " +
                    SerialNumberGenerator.Instance.NextSerial);
```

Part III. Structural Patterns

This part describes the seven structural patterns, that is, those that help manage how classes are organised and interrelate.

- *Adapter*: Convert the interface of a class into the interface clients expect, letting classes work together that couldn't otherwise because of incompatible types;

- *Bridge*: Decouple an abstraction from its implementation so that each may vary independently;

- *Composite*: Compose objects into tree structures to represent part-whole hierarchies, letting client objects treat individual objects and compositions uniformly;

- *Decorator*: Attach additional responsibilities to an object dynamically;

- *Façade*: Provide a uniform interface to a set of interfaces in a subsystem, by defining a higher-level interface that makes the subsystem easier to use;

- *Flyweight*: Use sharing to support large numbers of fine-grained objects efficiently;

- *Proxy*: Provide a surrogate or place-holder for another object to control access to it.

7. Adapter

Type	Structural
Purpose	Convert the interface of a class into another interface clients expect. *Adapter* lets classes work together that couldn't otherwise because of incompatible interfaces.

You will recall from the introduction that the Foobar Motor Company makes the engines for their vehicles. Here is a reminder of the IEngine hierarchy:

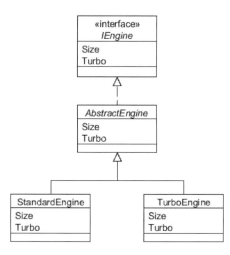

Figure 7.1 : IEngine class hierarchy

And here is a reminder of the code of the abstract AbstractEngine class:

```
public abstract class AbstractEngine : IEngine
{
    private int size;
    private bool turbo;

    public AbstractEngine(int size, bool turbo)
    {
        this.size = size;
```

```
            this.turbo = turbo;
        }

        public virtual int Size
        {
            get
            {
                return size;
            }
        }

        public virtual bool Turbo
        {
            get
            {
                return turbo;
            }
        }

        public override string ToString()
        {
            return this.GetType().Name + " (" + size + ")";
        }
    }
}
```

Let's say our client program takes engines stored in a collection and loops through them one at a time displaying the engine size and type:

```
IList<IEngine> engines = new List<IEngine>();

engines.Add(new StandardEngine(1300));
engines.Add(new StandardEngine(1600));
engines.Add(new TurboEngine(2000));

foreach (IEngine engine in engines)
{
    Console.WriteLine(engine);
}
Console.Read();
```

Running the above code would result in the following display:

```
StandardEngine (1300)
StandardEngine (1600)
TurboEngine (2000)
```

For this chapter we will assume that in addition to the two concrete subclasses (StandardEngine and TurboEngine) Foobar have decided to use a further engine class named `SuperGreenEngine` which is made by a different manufacturer.

Because the `SuperGreenEngine` class is provided by a third-party it does not implement our `IEngine` interface. Furthermore, Foobar do not have access to the C# source code and can therefore not modify it, but the following class details are known from the documentation:

• The class extends `object`;

• The constructor takes one argument for the engine size;

• There is an `EngineSize` property getter that returns the engine size as an `int`;

• These types of engines are never turbocharged;

• The `ToString()` method returns a string in the format: SUPER ENGINE nnnn (where nnnn is the engine size).

We can therefore see that `SuperGreenEngine` uses a different method name to access the engine size and there is no method related to whether it is turbocharged, and that it is not within the `IEngine` hierarchy. As it stands it would not be possible to add instances of `SuperGreenEngine` to the reporting collection and even if you could the method names are different.

The *Adapter* pattern provides an approach to resolve this through the definition of a new class that 'adapts' the class we want to use into the format existing classes require. For our purposes, therefore, we shall create a `SuperGreenEngineAdapter` class:

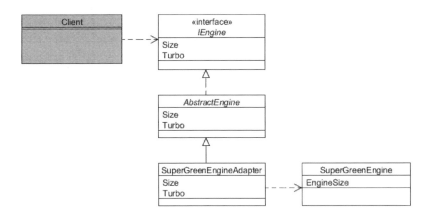

Figure 7.2 : Adapter class hierarchy

The code for the adapter is as follows:

```
public class SuperGreenEngineAdapter : AbstractEngine
{
    public SuperGreenEngineAdapter(SuperGreenEngine greenEngine)
            : base(greenEngine.EngineSize, false)
    {
    }
}
```

Note the following from the above code:

• We extend the class we are adapting **to**.

• We accept a reference in the constructor to the class we are adapting **from**.

• The constructor obtains the necessary state from the referenced object and passes it to the superclass constructor.

Now we are in a position to include SuperGreenEngine objects in our reporting collection (additional code indicated in bold):

```
IList<IEngine> engines = new List<IEngine>();

engines.Add(new StandardEngine(1300));
```

```
engines.Add(new StandardEngine(1600));
engines.Add(new TurboEngine(2000));

// "Adapt" the new engine type
SuperGreenEngine greenEngine = new SuperGreenEngine(1200);
engines.Add(new SuperGreenEngineAdapter(greenEngine));

// Unchanged from before...
foreach (IEngine engine in engines)
{
    Console.WriteLine(engine);
}
Console.Read();
```

The output should now be:

```
StandardEngine (1300)
StandardEngine (1600)
TurboEngine (2000)
SuperGreenEngineAdapter (1200)
```

Note how the output made use of the `ToString()` method as inherited from `AbstractEngine` rather than that of `SuperGreenEngine`.

Variations for implementing adapters

We were somewhat fortunate in that the design of the `AbstractEngine` and `SuperGreenEngine` classes made it easy for the adapter class to do the work inside its constructor. Often however, we need to take a few additional steps inside the code of the adapter class, so here is a general formula to apply:

1. Extend the class you are adapting to (or implement it, if it's an interface);

2. Specify the class you are adapting from in the constructor and store a reference to it in an instance variable;

3. For each method in the class you are extending (or interface you are implementing), override it to delegate to the corresponding method of the class you are adapting from.

Here is a generic example adapter class:

```
public class ObjectAdapter : ClassAdaptingTo
{
    private ClassAdaptingFrom fromObject;

    public ObjectAdapter(ClassAdaptingFrom fromObject)
    {
        this.fromObject = fromObject;
    }

    // Overridden method
    public override void MethodInToClass()
    {
        fromObject.MethodInFromClass();
    }
}
```

8. Bridge

Type	Structural
Purpose	Decouple an abstraction from its implementation so that each may vary independently.

The Foobar Motor Company manufactures engines for its vehicles. Here is a reminder of the IEngine class hierarchy:

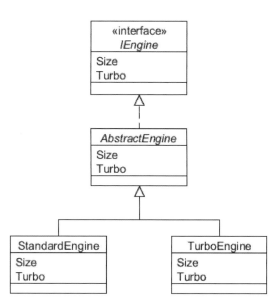

Figure 8.1 : IEngine class hierarchy

The implementation of the AbstractEngine class as detailed in the introduction, merely stores the engine size (e.g. 1600cc) and whether it is turbocharged. For the purposes of this chapter this class will be enhanced to enable the engine to be started and stopped and for the power to the engine to be increased or decreased.

The modified version of the `IEngine` interface and `AbstractEngine` class
is listed below with the changes marked in bold:

```
public interface IEngine
{
    int Size { get; }
    bool Turbo { get; }

    void Start();
    void Stop();
    void IncreasePower();
    void DecreasePower();
}
```

```
public abstract class AbstractEngine : IEngine
{
    private int size;
    private bool turbo;
    private bool running;
    private int power;

    public AbstractEngine(int size, bool turbo)
    {
        this.size = size;
        this.turbo = turbo;
        running = false;
        power = 0;
    }

    public virtual int Size
    {
        get
        {
            return size;
        }
    }

    public virtual bool Turbo
    {
        get
        {
            return turbo;
        }
    }

    public virtual void Start()
    {
        running = true;
    }

    public virtual void Stop()
    {
        running = false;
        power = 0;
```

```
    }

    public virtual void IncreasePower()
    {
        if ((running) && (power < 10))
        {
            power++;
        }
    }

    public virtual void DecreasePower()
    {
        if ((running) && (power > 0))
        {
            power--;
        }
    }

    public override string ToString()
    {
        return this.GetType().Name + " (" + size + ")";
    }
}
```

Within a vehicle, the driver controls the functions of the engine indirectly by means of various hand and foot controls, such as the ignition switch, accelerator pedal and brake pedal. To retain flexibility, it is important to design the connection between the engine and the controls so that each can vary independently of the other. In other words:

- *A new engine can be designed and plugged into a vehicle without needing any driver controls to be changed; and*

- *New driver controls (for example, to assist disabled drivers) can be designed and plugged into a vehicle without needing the engines to change.*

The *Bridge* pattern addresses this requirement by separating the 'abstraction' from the 'implementation' into two separate but connected hierarchies such that each can vary independently of the other. In our example, the 'abstraction' is the driver controls and the 'implementation' is the engine.

The following diagram shows this relationship:

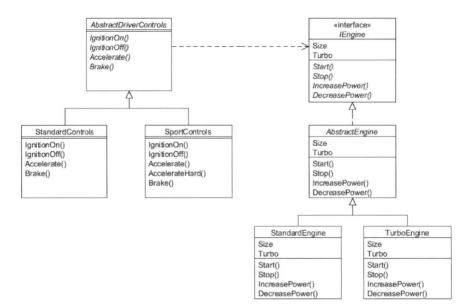

Figure 8.2 : Bridge pattern

As the above figure shows, there is an abstract `AbstractDriverControls` class with two concrete subclasses; `StandardControls` and `SportControls`:

The `AbstractDriverControls` class requires an `IEngine` object passed to its constructor and then delegates to the engine for each of its methods:

```
public abstract class AbstractDriverControls
{
    private IEngine engine;

    public AbstractDriverControls(IEngine engine)
    {
        this.engine = engine;
    }

    public virtual void IgnitionOn()
    {
        engine.Start();
    }

    public virtual void IgnitionOff()
    {
        engine.Stop();
    }
```

```
    public virtual void Accelerate()
    {
        engine.IncreasePower();
    }

    public virtual void Brake()
    {
        engine.DecreasePower();
    }
}
```

Subclasses of `AbstractDriverControls` can either use the superclass methods as-is or define additional functionality:

The `StandardControls` class extends `AbstractDriverControls` as-is:

```
public class StandardControls : AbstractDriverControls
{
    public StandardControls(IEngine engine) : base(engine) {
    }

    // No extra functions
}
```

Whereas the `SportControls` class defines an additional method:

```
public class SportControls : AbstractDriverControls
{
    public SportControls(IEngine engine) : base(engine) {
    }

    public virtual void AccelerateHard()
    {
        Accelerate();
        Accelerate();
    }
}
```

The important point to note from the above is that the additional method is coded in terms of the superclass 'abstraction' and *not* the 'implementation' (engine). So in the above example the `AccelerateHard()` method invokes the `Accelerate()` method as defined in `AbstractDriverControls`. It is this approach that allows the abstraction and the implementation to vary independently if needed.

Thus we could incorporate a brand-new type of engine without modifying the driver controls classes, provided the engine adheres to the `IEngine` contract. Conversely we could develop a new set of driver controls (such as enabling voice activation) without having to modify anything in the `IEngine` hierarchy.

Client programs can use the bridge as follows:

```
IEngine engine = new StandardEngine(1300);
StandardControls controls1 = new StandardControls(engine);
controls1.IgnitionOn();
controls1.Accelerate();
controls1.Nrake();
controls1.IgnitionOff();

// Now use sport controls
SportControls controls2 = new SportControls(engine);
controls2.IgnitionOn();
controls2.Accelerate();
controls2.AccelerateHard();
controls2.Brake();
controls2.IgnitionOff();
```

9. Composite

Type	Structural
Purpose	Compose objects into tree structures to represent part-whole hierarchies. *Composite* lets clients treat individual objects and compositions of objects uniformly.

In the Foobar Motor Company workshop they build various items from component parts such as nuts, bolts, panels, etc. Each individual component item has an associated description and unit cost, and when items are assembled into larger items the cost is therefore the sum of its component parts[1].

The *Composite* pattern enables us to treat both individual parts and assemblies of parts as if they are the same, thus enabling them to be processed in a consistent manner, simplifying code. The class hierarchy looks like this:

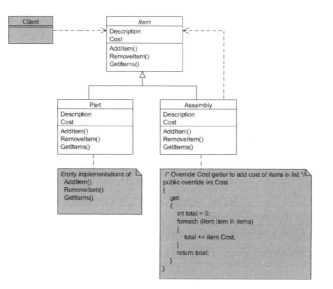

Figure 9.1 : Composite pattern

---

[1] We will ignore the cost of assembly, such as labour costs.

The abstract `Item` class defines all possible methods for both parts and assemblies of parts:

```csharp
public abstract class Item
{
    private string description;
    private int cost;

    public Item(string description, int cost)
    {
        this.description = description;
        this.cost = cost;
    }

    public virtual string Description
    {
        get
        {
            return description;
        }
    }

    public virtual int Cost
    {
        get
        {
            return cost;
        }
    }

    public abstract void AddItem(Item item);
    public abstract void RemoveItem(Item item);
    public abstract Item[] Items { get; }

    public override string ToString()
    {
        return description + " (cost " + Cost + ")";
    }
}
```

The above class provides default implementations for the `Description` `Cost` getters, and defines the abstract methods `AddItem()`, `RemoveItem()` and an `Items` property getter.

Individual parts are modelled using the `Part` subclass:

```csharp
public class Part : Item
{
    public Part(string description, int cost)
            : base(description, cost)
    {
```

```
    }

    // Empty implementations for unit parts...
    public override void AddItem(Item item)
    {
    }

    public override void RemoveItem(Item item)
    {
    }

    public override Item[] Items
    {
        get
        {
            return new Item[0];
        }
    }
}
```

As you can see, the methods related to managing assemblies of items have empty implementations since a 'part' is the smallest unit possible, and therefore unable to have sub-parts, unlike 'assemblies'.

Assemblies of parts are modelled using the Assembly subclass:

```
public class Assembly : Item
{
    private IList<Item> items;

    public Assembly(string description)
            : base(description, 0)
    {
        items = new List<Item>();
    }

    public override void AddItem(Item item)
    {
        items.Add(item);
    }

    public override void RemoveItem(Item item)
    {
        items.Remove(item);
    }

    public override Item[] Items
    {
        get
        {
            return items.ToArray();
        }
```

```
        }

        // Also have to override Cost getter to accumulate cost of all
        //  items in list
        public override int Cost
        {
            get
            {
                int total = 0;
                foreach (Item item in items)
                {
                    total += item.Cost;
                }
                return total;
            }
        }
    }
}
```

For assemblies, we have implemented the abstract methods to add other Item objects into an internal List collection. We have also overridden the Cost getter to loop through the collection to sum the cost of all contained items within this assembly.[1]

All types of Item objects can now be used in a uniform manner:

```
Item nut = new Part("Nut", 5);
Item bolt = new Part("Bolt", 9);
Item panel = new Part("Panel", 35);

Item gizmo = new Assembly("Gizmo");
gizmo.AddItem(panel);
gizmo.AddItem(nut);
gizmo.AddItem(bolt);

Item widget = new Assembly("Widget");
widget.AddItem(gizmo);
widget.AddItem(nut);
```

In the above extract, nuts, bolts and panels are defined as individual parts, a "Gizmo" is assembled from one nut, one bolt and one panel, and a "Widget" is assembled from one "Gizmo" and another nut.

Displaying the objects would result in this:

---

[1]We set the cost to zero when constructing Assembly object, since initially it has no component parts until they are added.

```
Nut (cost 5)
Bolt (cost 9)
Panel (cost 35)
Gizmo (cost 49)
Widget (cost 54)
```

The assemblies have computed the total cost without the client program needing to know how.

10. Decorator

Type	Structural
Purpose	Attach additional responsibilities to an object dynamically. Decorators provide a flexible alternative to sub-classing for extending functionality.

You will recall the Foobar Motor Company IVehicle class hierarchy:

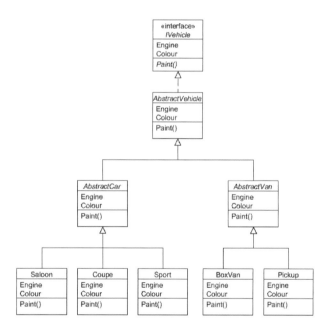

Figure 10.1 : IVehicle class hierarchy

For the purposes of this chapter, we shall add one additional property called Price to the IVehicle interface with a getter. We will also modify the ToString() method in AbstractVehicle to include the price. The modified interface and class is shown below with the changes marked in bold:

```
public interface IVehicle
```

```csharp
{
    IEngine Engine { get; }
    VehicleColour Colour { get; }
    void Paint(VehicleColour colour);

    int Price { get; }
}


public abstract class AbstractVehicle : IVehicle
{
    private IEngine engine;
    private VehicleColour colour;

    public AbstractVehicle(IEngine engine)
            : this(engine, VehicleColour.Unpainted)
    {
    }

    public AbstractVehicle(IEngine engine, VehicleColour colour)
    {
        this.engine = engine;
        this.colour = colour;
    }

    public virtual IEngine Engine
    {
        get
        {
            return engine;
        }
    }

    public virtual VehicleColour Colour
    {
        get
        {
            return colour;
        }
    }

    public virtual void Paint(VehicleColour colour)
    {
        this.colour = colour;
    }

    public abstract int Price { get; }

    public override string ToString()
    {
        return this.GetType().Name + " (" + engine + ", " + colour +
                                ", price " + Price + ")";
    }

}
```

Each of the concrete subclasses implements the `Price` getter as appropriate. For example, the `Saloon` class now looks like this (changes in bold):

```
public class Saloon : AbstractCar
{
    public Saloon(IEngine engine)
            : this(engine, VehicleColour.Unpainted)
    {
    }

    public Saloon(IEngine engine, VehicleColour colour)
            : base(engine, colour)
    {
    }

    public override int Price
    {
        get
        {
            return 6000;
        }
    }
}
```

The other subclasses are similarly defined, and the `Price` getter returns:

- 6,000 for `Saloon` objects;

- 7,000 for `Coupe` objects;

- 8,000 for `Sport` objects;

- 9,000 for `Pickup` objects;

- 10,000 for `BoxVan` objects.

When a customer buys a vehicle they have the choice of adding any number of optional extras. They can choose from an air-conditioning system, alloy wheels, leather seats, metallic paint, or a satellite-navigation unit. They can choose none at all, or any combination up to all five.

The *Decorator* pattern is designed to facilitate the addition of state and/or behaviour without having to modify the inheritance hierarchy of the classes being added to. This is accomplished by defining a new hierarchy which itself extends the root of the main tree.

This is shown diagrammatically below:

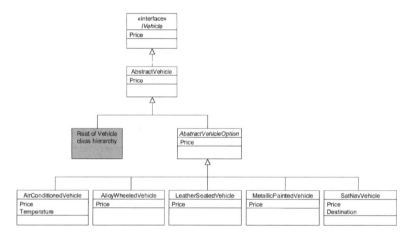

Figure 10.2 : Decorator pattern hierarchy

From the diagram you can see that a new abstract class has been defined called `AbstractVehicleOption` that inherits from `AbstractVehicle`. `AbstractVehicleOption` has five concrete subclasses; one for each option that can be selected.

The `AbstractVehicleOption` class looks like this:

```
public abstract class AbstractVehicleOption : AbstractVehicle
{
    protected internal IVehicle decoratedVehicle;

    public AbstractVehicleOption(IVehicle vehicle)
            : base(vehicle.Engine)
    {
        decoratedVehicle = vehicle;
    }
}
```

`AbstractVehicleOption` is the abstract "decorator" class and it requires a reference to the `IVehicle` class which is to be decorated.

Each of the option subclasses is straightforward. They all override the `Price` getter to add the price of the option to the price of the object that is being decorated. In the case of the `AirConditionedVehicle` and `SatNavVehicle` classes, we have also defined an extra method:

```
public class AirConditionedVehicle : AbstractVehicleOption
{
    public AirConditionedVehicle(IVehicle vehicle)
            : base(vehicle)
    {
    }

    public override int Price
    {
        get
        {
            return decoratedVehicle.Price + 600;
        }
    }

    public virtual int Temperature
    {
        set
        {
            // code to set the temperature...
        }
    }
}


public class AlloyWheeledVehicle : AbstractVehicleOption
{
    public AlloyWheeledVehicle(IVehicle vehicle)
            : base(vehicle)
    {
    }

    public override int Price
    {
        get
        {
            return decoratedVehicle.Price + 250;
        }
    }
}


public class LeatherSeatedVehicle : AbstractVehicleOption
{
```

```csharp
        public LeatherSeatedVehicle(IVehicle vehicle)
                : base(vehicle)
        {
        }

        public override int Price
        {
            get
            {
                return decoratedVehicle.Price + 1200;
            }
        }
    }



    public class MetallicPaintedVehicle : AbstractVehicleOption
    {
        public MetallicPaintedVehicle(IVehicle vehicle)
                : base(vehicle)
        {
        }

        public override int Price
        {
            get
            {
                return decoratedVehicle.Price + 750;
            }
        }
    }



    public class SatNavVehicle : AbstractVehicleOption
    {
        public SatNavVehicle(IVehicle vehicle)
                : base(vehicle)
        {
        }

        public override int Price
        {
            get
            {
                return decoratedVehicle.Price + 1500;
            }
        }

        public virtual string Destination
        {
            set
            {
                // code to set the destination...
            }
        }
    }
```

To use the 'decorators' we initially instantiate the car or van we require and then "wrap" them inside the required decorator or decorators.

Here is an example:

```
// Create a blue saloon car
IVehicle myCar = new Saloon(new StandardEngine(1300));
myCar.Paint(VehicleColour.Blue);

// Add air-conditioning to the car...
myCar = new AirConditionedVehicle(myCar);

// Now add alloy wheels...
myCar = new AlloyWheeledVehicle(myCar);

// Now add leather seats...
myCar = new LeatherSeatedVehicle(myCar);

// Now add metallic paint...
myCar = new MetallicPaintedVehicle(myCar);

// Now add satellite navigation
myCar = new SatNavVehicle(myCar);
```

If you invoke `Console.WriteLine` on the `myCar` object at each stage you should see this output:

```
Saloon (StandardEngine (1300), Blue, price 6000)
AirConditionedVehicle (StandardEngine (1300), Blue, price 6600)
AlloyWheeledVehicle (StandardEngine (1300), Blue, price 6850)
LeatherSeatedVehicle (StandardEngine (1300), Blue, price 8050)
MetallicPaintedVehicle (StandardEngine (1300), Blue, price 8800)
SatNavVehicle (StandardEngine (1300), Blue, price 10300)
```

The price shown at each stage is the total of the vehicle plus the selected options as each is "added".

The *Decorator* pattern is a good example of preferring object composition over inheritance. Had we attempted to use inheritance for the various vehicle options we would have needed to create many different combinations of subclasses to model each combination of selectable options.

Decorator classes are sometimes called "wrapper" classes, since they serve to "wrap" an object inside another object, usually to add or modify its functionality.

11. Facade

Type	Structural
Purpose	Provide a unified interface to a set of interfaces in a subsystem. *Facade* defines a higher-level interface that makes the subsystem easier to use.

Sometimes you need to perform a series of steps to undertake a particular task, often involving multiple objects. The *Facade* pattern involves the creation of a separate object that simplifies the execution of such steps.

As an example, when the Foobar Motor Company are preparing their vehicles for sale there are a number of steps they have to undertake that utilise various objects. In this chapter we shall assume that the `IVehicle` interface defines the following additional methods beyond those defined in the introduction.

```
// Extra methods defined in IVehicle...

void CleanInterior();
void CleanExteriorBody();
void PolishWindows();
void TakeForTestDrive();
```

The above methods are implemented in `AbstractVehicle` as follows:

```
public virtual void CleanInterior()
{
    Console.WriteLine("Cleaning interior...");
}

public virtual void CleanExteriorBody()
{
    Console.WriteLine("Cleaning exterior body...");
}

public virtual void PolishWindows()
{
    Console.WriteLine("Polishing windows...");
}

public virtual void TakeForTestDrive()
```

```
    {
        Console.WriteLine("Taking for test drive...");
    }
```

We shall introduce two further simple classes called `Registration` and `Documentation`:

```
public class Registration
{
    private IVehicle vehicle;

    public Registration(IVehicle vehicle)
    {
        this.vehicle = vehicle;
    }

    public virtual void AllocateLicensePlate()
    {
        Console.WriteLine("Allocating license plate...");
    }

    public virtual void AllocateVehicleNumber()
    {
        Console.WriteLine("Allocating vehicle number...");
    }
}


public class Documentation
{
    public static void PrintBrochure(IVehicle vehicle)
    {
        Console.WriteLine("Printing brochure...");
    }
}
```

To implement the pattern we will create a `VehicleFacade` class that defines a method to prepare the specified vehicle by using the above classes on our behalf:

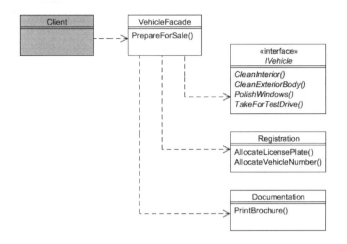

Figure 11.1 : Facade pattern

```
public class VehicleFacade
{
    public virtual void PrepareForSale(IVehicle vehicle)
    {
        Registration reg = new Registration(vehicle);
        reg.AllocateVehicleNumber();
        reg.AllocateLicensePlate();

        Documentation.PrintBrochure(vehicle);

        vehicle.CleanInterior();
        vehicle.CleanExteriorBody();
        vehicle.PolishWindows();
        vehicle.TakeForTestDrive();
    }
}
```

Client programs then only need invoke the `PrepareForSale()` method on a `VehicleFacade` instance, and therefore need no knowledge of what needs to be done and what other objects are needed. And if something different is needed in a special circumstance, then the individual methods are still available for calling as required.

12. Flyweight

Type	Structural
Purpose	Use sharing to support large numbers of fine-grained objects efficiently.

Some programs need to create a large number of objects of one particular type, and if those objects happen to have a large amount of state then instantiating lots of them can quickly use up memory. When considering object state, we often note that at least some of it could potentially be shared among a group of objects.

For the Foobar Motor Company, the IEngine hierarchy is a case in point:

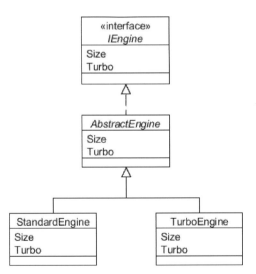

Figure 12.1 : IEngine class hierarchy

Our simple implementation of IEngine only defines two property getters; Size and Turbo. Let's suppose we instantiate two engines as follows:

```
Engine engine1 = new StandardEngine(1300);
Engine engine2 = new StandardEngine(1300);
```

The above would create two separate objects in memory, even though their state is identical. This can be thought of as its *intrinsic state*; i.e. all 1300cc standard engines will be storing *1300* for the engine size and `false` for whether it is turbocharged. Creating hundreds or thousands of these would be wasteful of memory, especially since a more realistic `Engine` class would require many more variables whose values would also be shared.

For the purposes of this chapter another method will be added to the `IEngine` interface, called `Diagnose()`. This new method will take an `IDiagnosticTool` object as its argument, and this argument can be thought of as its *extrinsic state*, since its value is not actually stored in the `IEngine` object – it is used purely so that the engine can use it to run a diagnostic check.

The `IDiagnosticTool` interface looks like this:

```
public interface IDiagnosticTool
{
    void RunDiagnosis(object obj);
}
```

The `EngineDiagnosticTool` implements the above for running diagnostics on an engine:

```
public class EngineDiagnosticTool : IDiagnosticTool
{
    public virtual void RunDiagnosis(object obj)
    {
        Console.WriteLine("Starting engine diagnostic tool for "
                                                    + obj);
        Thread.Sleep(5000);
        Console.WriteLine("Engine diagnosis complete");
    }
}
```

To simulate a long-running process the method pauses for five seconds.

With the above in place we can now add a suitable method to the `Engine` interface:

```
public interface IEngine {

    // Properties having intrinsic (i.e. shared) state
    int Size { get; }
    bool Turbo { get; }

    // Methods having extrinsic (i.e. unshared) state
    void Diagnose(IDiagnosticTool tool);
}
```

The implementation of this new method in `AbstractEngine` simply issues a call-back to the `IDiagnosticTool`:

```
public virtual void Diagnose(IDiagnosticTool tool)
{
    tool.RunDiagnosis(this);
}
```

The *Flyweight* pattern allows you to reference a multitude of objects of the same type and having the same state, but only by instantiating the minimum number of actual objects needed. This is typically done by allocating a 'pool' of objects which can be shared, and this is determined by a 'flyweight factory' class. Client programs get access to engines only through the factory:

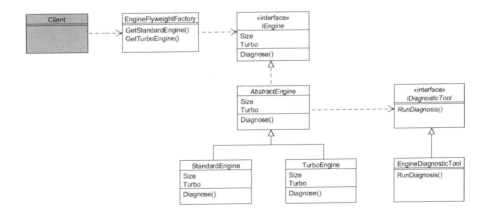

Figure 12.2 : Flyweight pattern

The `EngineFlyweightFactory` class looks like this:

```
public class EngineFlyweightFactory
{
    private IDictionary<int?, IEngine> standardEnginePool;
    private IDictionary<int?, IEngine> turboEnginePool;

    public EngineFlyweightFactory()
    {
        standardEnginePool = new Dictionary<int?, IEngine>();
        turboEnginePool = new Dictionary<int?, IEngine>();
    }

    public virtual IEngine GetStandardEngine(int size)
    {
        IEngine e = null;
        bool found = standardEnginePool.TryGetValue(size, out e);
        if (! found)
        {
            e = new StandardEngine(size);
            standardEnginePool[size] = e;
        }
        return e;
    }

    public virtual IEngine GetTurboEngine(int size)
    {
        IEngine e = null;
        bool found = turboEnginePool.TryGetValue(size, out e);
        if (!found)
        {
            e = new TurboEngine(size);
            turboEnginePool[size] = e;
        }
        return e;
    }
}
```

This class utilises two dictionaries (one for standard engines and the other for turbo engines). Each time an engine of a particular type and size is requested, if a similar one has already been created it is returned rather than instantiating a new one.

Client programs use the factory like this:

```
// Create the flyweight factory...
EngineFlyweightFactory factory = new EngineFlyweightFactory();
```

```
// Create the diagnostic tool
IDiagnosticTool tool = new EngineDiagnosticTool();

// Get the flyweights and run diagnostics on them
IEngine standard1 = factory.GetStandardEngine(1300);
standard1.Diagnose(tool);

IEngine standard2 = factory.GetStandardEngine(1300);
standard2.Diagnose(tool);

IEngine standard3 = factory.GetStandardEngine(1300);
standard3.Diagnose(tool);

IEngine standard4 = factory.GetStandardEngine(1600);
standard4.Diagnose(tool);

IEngine standard5 = factory.GetStandardEngine(1600);
standard5.Diagnose(tool);

// Show that objects are shared
Console.WriteLine(standard1.GetHashCode());
Console.WriteLine(standard2.GetHashCode());
Console.WriteLine(standard3.GetHashCode());
Console.WriteLine(standard4.GetHashCode());
Console.WriteLine(standard5.GetHashCode());
Console.Read();
```

In the above, the variables standard1, standard2 and standard3 all reference the same IEngine object (since they all 1300cc standard engines). Likewise, standard4 references the same object as standard5. Of course, whether it is worth running the diagnostics multiple times on the same objects is arguable depending upon the circumstances!

If the arguments passed to the extrinsic method (IDiagnosticTool in our example) need to be stored, this should be done in the client program.

13. Proxy

Type	Structural
Purpose	Provide a surrogate or place-holder for another object to control access to it.

Some methods can be time-consuming, such as those that load complex graphical components or need network connections. In these instances, the *Proxy* pattern provides a 'stand-in' object until such time that the time-consuming resource is complete, allowing the rest of your application to load.

In the chapter discussing the *Flyweight* pattern, the IEngine hierarchy was enhanced to define the additional method Diagnose(). As you saw, the implementation of RunDiagnosis() in EngineDiagnosticTool is slow (we made it sleep for five seconds to simulate this), so we might consider making this run is a separate thread.

Here is a reminder of the Engine hierarchy with the additional method:

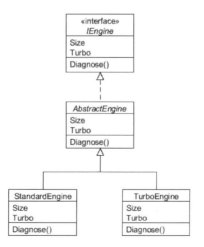

Figure 13.1 : IEngine class hierarchy

The *Proxy* pattern involves creating a class that implements the same interface that we are standing-in for, in our case `IEngine`. The proxy then forwards requests to the "real" object which it stores internally. Clients just access the proxy:

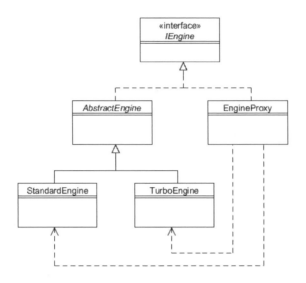

Figure 13.2 : Proxy pattern

Here is the code for the `EngineProxy` class:

```
public class EngineProxy : IEngine
{
    private IEngine engine;

    public EngineProxy(int size, bool turbo)
    {
        if (turbo)
        {
            engine = new TurboEngine(size);
        }
        else
        {
            engine = new StandardEngine(size);
        }
    }

    public virtual int Size
    {
        get
        {
```

```
            return engine.Size;
        }
    }

    public virtual bool Turbo
    {
        get
        {
            return engine.Turbo;
        }
    }

    // This method is time-consuming...
    public virtual void Diagnose(IDiagnosticTool tool)
    {
        Console.WriteLine("(Running tool as thread)");
        Thread t = new Thread(() => RunDiagnosticTool(tool));
        t.Start();
        Console.WriteLine("EngineProxy diagnose() method finished");
    }

    public virtual void RunDiagnosticTool(IDiagnosticTool tool)
    {
        tool.RunDiagnosis(this);
    }
}
```

The constructor creates either a `StandardEngine` or `TurboEngine` object and stores a reference to it as an instance variable. Calls to the `Size` and `Turbo` getters simply forward to the referenced engine object. Calls to `Diagnose()` will invoke a separate thread to run the actual diagnosis.

Part IV. Behavioural Patterns

This part describes the eleven behavioural patterns, that is, those that help manage what the classes actually do.

- *Chain of Responsibility*: Avoid coupling the sender of a request to its receiver by giving more than one object the chance to handle the request;

- *Command*: Encapsulate a request as an object, thereby letting you parameterise clients with different requests;

- *Interpreter*: Define the representation of a language's grammar;

- *Iterator*: Provide a way to access the elements of an aggregate object sequentially without exposing its underlying representation;

- *Mediator*: Define an object that encapsulates how a set of objects interact;

- *Memento*: Capture and externalise an object's state so that it can be restored to that state later;

- *Observer*: Define a one-to-many dependency between objects so that when one object changes its state, all of its dependents are notified and updated automatically;

- *State*: Allow an object to alter its behaviour when its internal state changes, as if it were a different class;

- *Strategy*: Allow clients to change the algorithm that an object uses to perform a function;

- *Template Method*: Define the skeleton of an algorithm in a method, deferring some steps to subclasses;

- *Visitor*. Simulate the addition of a method to a class without needing to actually change the class.

14. Chain of Responsibility

Type	Behavioural
Purpose	Avoid coupling the sender of a request to its receiver by giving more than one object a chance to handle the request. Chain the receiving objects and pass the request along the chain until an object handles it.

The Foobar Motor Company receives many emails each day, including servicing requests, sales enquiries, complaints, and of course the inevitable spam. Rather than employ someone specifically to sort through each email to determine which department it should be forwarded to, our task is to try and automate this by analysing the text in each email and making a "best guess".

In our simplified example, we will search the text of the email for a number of keywords and depending upon what we find will process accordingly. Here are the words we will search for and how they should be handled:

Keywords	Forward to
"viagra", "pills", "medicines"	Spam handler
"buy", "purchase"	Sales department
"service", "repair"	Servicing department
"complain", "bad"	Manager
Anything else...	General enquiries

Note that only one object needs to handle the request, so if a particular email contains both "purchase" and "repair" it will be forwarded to the sales department only. The sequence in which to check the keywords is whatever seems most sensible for the application; so here we are trying to filter out spam before it reaches any other department.

Now it would be possible, of course, to just have a series of `if...else...` statements when checking for the keywords, but that would not be very object-oriented. The *Chain of Responsibility* pattern instead allows us to define separate 'handler' objects that all conform to an `IEmailHandler` interface. This enables us to keep each handler independent and loosely-coupled.

The following diagram shows the pattern:

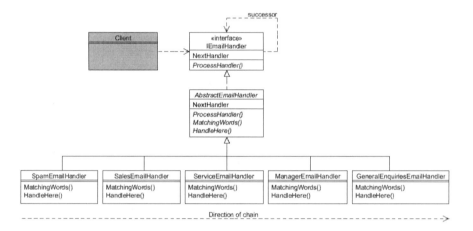

Figure 14.1 : Chain of Responsibility pattern

`IEmailHandler` is the interface at the top of the hierarchy:

```
public interface IEmailHandler
{
    IEmailHandler NextHandler { set; }
    void ProcessHandler(string email);
}
```

The `NextHandler` setter takes another `IEmailHandler` object as its argument which represents the handler to call if the current object is unable to handle the email.

The `ProcessHandler()` method takes the email text as its argument and determines if it is able to handle it (i.e. if it contains one of the keywords we are interested in). If the active object can handle the email it does so, otherwise it just forwards to the next in the chain.

The `AbstractEmailHandler` class implements the `IEmailHandler` interface to provide useful default functionality:

```
public abstract class AbstractEmailHandler : IEmailHandler
{
    private IEmailHandler nextHandler;

    public virtual IEmailHandler NextHandler
    {
        set
        {
            nextHandler = value;
        }
    }

    public virtual void ProcessHandler(string email)
    {
        bool wordFound = false;
        // If no words to match against then this object can handle
        if (MatchingWords().Length == 0)
        {
            wordFound = true;
        }
        else
        {
            // Look for any of the matching words
            foreach (string word in MatchingWords())
            {
                if (email.IndexOf(word) >= 0)
                {
                    wordFound = true;
                    break;
                }
            }
        }

        // Can we handle email in this object?
        if (wordFound)
        {
            HandleHere(email);
        }
        else
        {
            // Unable to handle here so forward to next in chain
            nextHandler.ProcessHandler(email);
        }
    }
```

```
        protected internal abstract string[] MatchingWords();
        protected internal abstract void HandleHere(string email);
    }
```

The `NextHandler` setter simply stores the argument in an instance variable; the decision making process is made in `ProcessHandler()`. This has been written to utilise two `protected` helper methods that must be implemented by concrete subclasses:

- `MatchingWords()` will return an array of `string` objects that this handler is interested in;

- `HandleHere()` is only called if this object can actually handle the email and contains whatever code is required.

The concrete subclasses are straightforward:

```
public class SpamEmailHandler : AbstractEmailHandler
{
    protected internal override string[] MatchingWords()
    {
        return new string[] { "viagra", "pills", "medicines" };
    }

    protected internal override void HandleHere(string email)
    {
        Console.WriteLine("This is a spam email.");
    }
}

public class SalesEmailHandler : AbstractEmailHandler
{
    protected internal override string[] MatchingWords()
    {
        return new string[] { "buy", "purchase" };
    }

    protected internal override void HandleHere(string email)
    {
        Console.WriteLine("Email handled by sales department.");
    }
}

public class ServiceEmailHandler : AbstractEmailHandler
{
    protected internal override string[] MatchingWords()
```

```
        {
            return new string[] { "service", "repair" };
        }

        protected internal override void HandleHere(string email)
        {
            Console.WriteLine("Email handled by service department.");
        }
    }

    public class ManagerEmailHandler : AbstractEmailHandler
    {
        protected internal override string[] MatchingWords()
        {
            return new string[] { "complain", "bad" };
        }

        protected internal override void HandleHere(string email)
        {
            Console.WriteLine("Email handled by manager.");
        }
    }

    public class GeneralEnquiriesEmailHandler : AbstractEmailHandler
    {
        protected internal override string[] MatchingWords()
        {
            return new string[0]; // match anything
        }

        protected internal override void HandleHere(string email)
        {
            Console.WriteLine("Email handled by general enquires.");
        }
    }
```

We now need to define the sequence in which the handlers are called. For this example, the following `static` method has been added to `AbstractEmailHandler`:

```
    public static void Handle(string email)
    {
        // Create the handler objects...
        IEmailHandler spam = new SpamEmailHandler();
        IEmailHandler sales = new SalesEmailHandler();
        IEmailHandler service = new ServiceEmailHandler();
        IEmailHandler manager = new ManagerEmailHandler();
        IEmailHandler general = new GeneralEnquiriesEmailHandler();

        // Chain them together...
        spam.NextHandler = sales;
        sales.NextHandler = service;
        service.NextHandler = manager;
```

```
    manager.NextHandler = general;

    // Start the ball rolling...
    spam.ProcessHandler(email);
}
```

Putting a message through the handlers is now as simple as this:

```
string email = "I need my car repaired";
AbstractEmailHandler.Handle(email);
Console.Read();
```

This should produce the following output:

```
Email handled by service department.
```

15. Command

Type	Behavioural
Purpose	Encapsulate a request as an object, thereby letting you parameterise clients with different requests, queue or log requests, and support undoable operations.

The vehicles made by the Foobar Motor Company each have an installed radio; this is modelled by the following `Radio` class:

```
public class Radio
{
    public const int MinVolume = 0;
    public const int MaxVolume = 10;
    public const int DefaultVolume = 5;

    private bool switchedOn;
    private int volume;

    public Radio()
    {
        switchedOn = false;
        volume = DefaultVolume;
    }

    public virtual bool On
    {
        get
        {
            return switchedOn;
        }
    }

    public virtual int Volume
    {
        get
        {
            return volume;
        }
    }

    public virtual void SwitchOn()
    {
        switchedOn = true;
        Console.WriteLine("Radio now on, volume level " + Volume);
    }

    public virtual void SwitchOff()
```

```
    {
        switchedOn = false;
        Console.WriteLine("Radio now off");
    }

    public virtual void VolumeUp()
    {
        if (On)
        {
            if (Volume < MaxVolume)
            {
                volume++;
                Console.WriteLine("Volume turned up to level "
                                            + Volume);
            }
        }
    }

    public virtual void VolumeDown()
    {
        if (On)
        {
            if (Volume > MinVolume)
            {
                volume--;
                Console.WriteLine("Volume turned down to level "
                                            + Volume);
            }
        }
    }
}
```

As you can see, the class enables the radio to be switched on and off, and provided it is switched on will enable the volume to be increased or decreased one level at a time, within the range 1 to 10[1].

Some of the vehicles also have electrically operated windows with simple up & down buttons, as modelled by the following ElectricWindow class[2].

```
public class ElectricWindow
{
    private bool open;

    public ElectricWindow()
    {
        open = false;
```

---

[1]The code to set the station frequency has been omitted.
[2]For simplicity the windows can only be either fully open or fully closed.

```csharp
            Console.WriteLine("Window is closed");
    }

    public virtual bool Open
    {
        get
        {
            return open;
        }
    }

    public virtual bool Closed
    {
        get
        {
            return (!open);
        }
    }

    public virtual void OpenWindow()
    {
        if (Closed)
        {
            open = true;
            Console.WriteLine("Window is now open");
        }
    }

    public virtual void CloseWindow()
    {
        if (Open)
        {
            open = false;
            Console.WriteLine("Window is now closed");
        }
    }
}
```

Each of the devices (the radio and the electric window) has separate controls, typically buttons, to manage their state. But suppose the Foobar Motor Company now wishes to introduce speech recognition to their top-of-the-range vehicles and have them perform as follows:

- *If the speech-recognition system is in "radio" mode, then if it hears the word "up" or "down" it adjusts the radio volume; or*

- *If the speech-recognition system is in "window" mode, then if it hears the word "up" or "down" it closes or opens the driver's door window.*

We therefore need the speech-recognition system to be able to handle either `Radio` objects or `ElectricWindow` objects, which are of course in completely separate hierarchies. We might also want it to handle other devices in the future, such as the vehicle's speed or the gearbox (e.g. upon hearing "up" it would increase the speed by 1mph or it would change to the next higher gear). For good object-oriented design we need to isolate the speech-recognition from the devices it controls, so it can cope with any device without directly knowing what they are.

The *Command* patterns allows us to uncouple an object making a request from the object that receives the request and performs the action, by means of a "middle-man" object known as a "command object".

In its simplest form, this requires us to create an interface (which we shall call `IVoiceCommand`) with one method:

```
public interface IVoiceCommand
{
    void Execute();
}
```

We now need to create implementing classes for each action that we wish to take[1]. For example, to turn up the volume of the radio we can create a `VolumeUpCommand` class:

```
public class VolumeUpCommand : IVoiceCommand
{
    private Radio radio;

    public VolumeUpCommand(Radio radio)
    {
        this.radio = radio;
    }

    public virtual void Execute()
    {
        radio.VolumeUp();
    }
}
```

---

[1]The *Command* pattern is sometimes known as the *Action* pattern.

The class simply takes a reference to a `Radio` object in its constructor and invokes its `VolumeUp()` method whenever `Execute()` is called.

We likewise need to create a `VolumeDownCommand` class for when the volume is to be reduced:

```
public class VolumeDownCommand : IVoiceCommand
{
    private Radio radio;

    public VolumeUpCommand(Radio radio)
    {
        this.radio = radio;
    }

    public virtual void Execute()
    {
        radio.VolumeDown();
    }
}
```

Controlling an electric window's up and down movement is just as easy: this time we create classes implementing `IVoiceCommand` passing in a reference to an `ElectricWindow` object:

```
public class WindowUpCommand : IVoiceCommand
{
    private ElectricWindow window;

    public WindowUpCommand(ElectricWindow window)
    {
        this.window = window;
    }

    public virtual void Execute()
    {
        window.CloseWindow();
    }
}


public class WindowDownCommand : IVoiceCommand
{
    private ElectricWindow window;

    public WindowUpCommand(ElectricWindow window)
    {
        this.window = window;
    }

    public virtual void Execute()
```

```
        {
            window.OpenWindow();
        }
    }
```

We will now define a `SpeechRecogniser` class that only knows about `IVoiceCommand` objects – it knows nothing about radios or electric windows.

```
    public class SpeechRecogniser
    {
        private IVoiceCommand upCommand, downCommand;

        public virtual void SetCommands(IVoiceCommand upCommand,
                                        IVoiceCommand downCommand)
        {
            this.upCommand = upCommand;
            this.downCommand = downCommand;
        }

        public virtual void HearUpSpoken()
        {
            upCommand.Execute();
        }

        public virtual void HearDownSpoken()
        {
            downCommand.Execute();
        }
    }
```

We can view what we have created diagrammatically as follows:

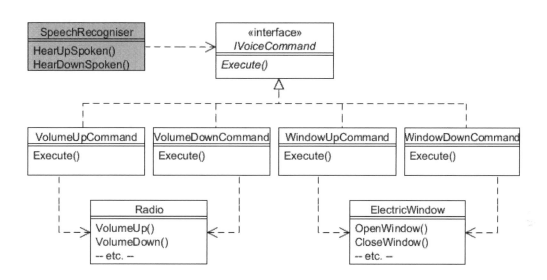

Figure 15.1 : Command pattern

Client programs can now create `Radio` and `ElectricWindow` instances, along with their respective `IVoiceCommand` instances. The command instances are then passed to the `SpeechRecogniser` object so it knows what to do.

We will first create a `Radio` and an `ElectricWindow` and their respective commands:

```
// Create a radio and its up/down command objects
Radio radio = new Radio();
radio.SwitchOn();
IVoiceCommand volumeUpCommand = new VolumeUpCommand(radio);
IVoiceCommand volumeDownCommand = new VolumeDownCommand(radio);

// Create an electric window and its up/down command objects
ElectricWindow window = new ElectricWindow();
IVoiceCommand windowUpCommand = new WindowUpCommand(window);
```

```
IVoiceCommand windowDownCommand = new WindowDownCommand(window);
```

Now create a single `SpeechRecogniser` object and set it to control the radio:

```
// Create a speech recogniser object
SpeechRecogniser speechRecogniser = new SpeechRecogniser();
speechRecogniser.SetCommands(volumeUpCommand, volumeDownCommand);
Console.WriteLine("Speech recognition controlling the radio");
speechRecogniser.HearUpSpoken();
speechRecogniser.HearUpSpoken();
speechRecogniser.HearUpSpoken();
speechRecogniser.HearDownSpoken();
```

Now set the *same* `SpeechRecogniser` object to control the window instead:

```
speechRecogniser.SetCommands(windowUpCommand, windowDownCommand);
Console.WriteLine("Speech recognition will now control the window");
speechRecogniser.HearDownSpoken();
speechRecogniser.HearUpSpoken();

Console.Read();
```

If you run all the above statements you should see output similar to this:

```
Radio now on, volume level 5
Window is closed
Speech recognition controlling the radio
Volume turned up to level 6
Volume turned up to level 7
Volume turned up to level 8
Volume turned down to level 7
Speech recognition will now control the window
Window is now open
Window is now closed
```

Typical uses of the Command Pattern

One of the most frequent uses of the *Command* pattern is in UI toolkits. These provide pre-built components like graphical buttons and menu items that cannot possibly know what needs to be done when clicked, because that is always specific to your application.

Another common aspect of graphical applications is the provision of an "undo" mechanism. The *Command* pattern is used to accomplish this too; using the example in this chapter, we would add a method to the IVoiceCommand interface like this:

```
public interface IVoiceCommand
{
    void Execute();
    void Undo();
}
```

Implementing classes then provide the code for the additional method to reverse the last action, as in this example for the VolumeUpCommand class:

```
public class VolumeUpCommand : IVoiceCommand
{
    private Radio radio;

    public VolumeUpCommand(Radio radio)
    {
        this.radio = radio;
    }

    public virtual void Execute()
    {
        radio.VolumeUp();
    }

    public virtual void Undo()
    {
        radio.VolumeDown();
    }

}
```

Most applications would be slightly more involved than the above example, in that you would need to store the state of the object prior to performing the code in the Execute() method, enabling you to restore that state when Undo() is called.

16. Interpreter

Type	Behavioural
Purpose	Given a language, define a representation for its grammar along with an interpreter that uses the representation to interpret sentences in the language.

The satellite-navigation systems fitted to some of the Foobar Motor Company's vehicles have a special feature that enables the user to enter a number of cities and let it calculate the most northerly, southerly, westerly or easterly, depending on which command string is entered. A sample command might look like this:

```
london edinburgh manchester southerly
```

The above would result in "London" being returned, being the most southerly of the three entered cities. You can even enter the command string like this:

```
london edinburgh manchester southerly aberdeen westerly
```

This would first determine that London was the most southerly and then use that result (London) and compare it to Aberdeen to tell you which of those two is the most westerly[1]. Any number of cities can be entered before each of the directional commands of "northerly", "southerly", "westerly" and "easterly".

You can think of the above command string consisting of the city names and directional keywords as forming a simple "language" that needs to be interpreted by the satellite-navigation software. The *Interpreter* pattern is

---

[1] It's Aberdeen.

an approach that helps to decipher these kinds of relatively simple languages.

Before looking at the pattern itself, we shall create a class named `City` which models the essential points of interest for our example, which is just the name of the city and its latitude and longitude:

```
public class City
{
    private string name;
    private double latitude, longitude;

    public City(string name, double latitude, double longitude)
    {
        this.name = name;
        this.latitude = latitude;
        this.longitude = longitude;
    }

    public virtual string Name
    {
        get
        {
            return name;
        }
    }

    public virtual double Latitude
    {
        get
        {
            return latitude;
        }
    }

    public virtual double Longitude
    {
        get
        {
            return longitude;
        }
    }

    public override bool Equals(object otherObject)
    {
        if (this == otherObject)
        {
            return true;
        }
        if (!(otherObject is City))
        {
            return false;
        }
        City otherCity = (City)otherObject;
```

```
        return Name.Equals(otherCity.Name);
    }

    public override int GetHashCode()
    {
        return Name.GetHashCode();
    }

    public override string ToString()
    {
        return Name;
    }
}
```

You will notice that for simplicity the latitude and longitude are stored as doubles. Also note that for the latitude positive values represent North and negative values represent South. Similarly, a positive longitude represents East and negative values West. The example in this chapter only includes a small number of UK cities which are all Northern latitude and Western longitude, although any city should work should you wish to use your own.

The classes to interpret the language are structured as follows:

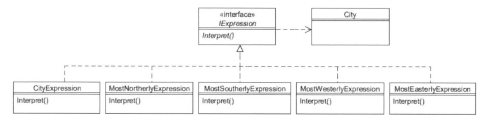

Figure 16.1 : Interpreter pattern

The *Interpreter* pattern resembles the *Composite* pattern in that it comprises an interface (or abstract class) with two types of concrete subclass; one type that represents the individual elements and the other type that represents repeating elements. We create one subclass to handle each type of element in the language.

The IExpression interface is very simple, merely declaring an Interpret() method that returns a City object:

```
public interface IExpression
{
    City Interpret();
}
```

The first concrete subclass we will look at is CityExpression, an instance of which will be created for each city name it recognises in the command string. All this class needs to do is store a reference to a City object and return it when Interpret() is invoked:

```
public class CityExpression : IExpression
{
    private City city;

    public CityExpression(City city)
    {
        this.city = city;
    }

    public virtual City Interpret()
    {
        return city;
    }
}
```

The classes to handle each of the commands (e.g. "northerly") are slightly more involved:

```
public class MostNortherlyExpression : IExpression
{
    private IList<IExpression> expressions;

    public MostNortherlyExpression(IList<IExpression> expressions)
    {
        this.expressions = expressions;
    }

    public virtual City Interpret()
    {
        City resultingCity = new City("Nowhere", -999.9, -999.9);
        foreach (IExpression currentExpression in expressions)
        {
            City currentCity = currentExpression.Interpret();
            if (currentCity.Latitude > resultingCity.Latitude)
            {
```

```
                resultingCity = currentCity;
            }
        }
        return resultingCity;
    }
}
```

The list of `IExpression` objects passed to the constructor will be of the `CityExpression` type. The `Interpret()` method loops through each of these to determine the most northerly, by comparing their latitude values.

The `MostSoutherlyExpression` class is very similar, merely changing the comparison:

```
public class MostSoutherlyExpression : IExpression
{
    private IList<IExpression> expressions;

    public MostSoutherlyExpression(IList<IExpression> expressions)
    {
        this.expressions = expressions;
    }

    public virtual City Interpret()
    {
        City resultingCity = new City("Nowhere", 999.9, 999.9);
        foreach (IExpression currentExpression in expressions)
        {
            City currentCity = currentExpression.Interpret();
            if (currentCity.Latitude < resultingCity.Latitude)
            {
                resultingCity = currentCity;
            }
        }
        return resultingCity;
    }
}
```

Likewise the `MostWesterlyExpression` and `MostEasterlyExpression` classes compute and return the appropriate `City`:

```
public class MostWesterlyExpression : IExpression
{
    private IList<IExpression> expressions;

    public MostWesterlyExpression(IList<IExpression> expressions)
    {
        this.expressions = expressions;
    }
```

```
    public virtual City Interpret()
    {
        City resultingCity = new City("Nowhere", 999.9, 999.9);
        foreach (IExpression currentExpression in expressions)
        {
            City currentCity = currentExpression.Interpret();
            if (currentCity.Longitude < resultingCity.Longitude)
            {
                resultingCity = currentCity;
            }
        }
        return resultingCity;
    }
}


public class MostEasterlyExpression : IExpression
{
    private IList<IExpression> expressions;

    public MostEasterlyExpression(IList<IExpression> expressions)
    {
        this.expressions = expressions;
    }

    public virtual City Interpret()
    {
        City resultingCity = new City("Nowhere", -999.9, -999.9);
        foreach (IExpression currentExpression in expressions)
        {
            City currentCity = currentExpression.Interpret();
            if (currentCity.Longitude > resultingCity.Longitude)
            {
                resultingCity = currentCity;
            }
        }
        return resultingCity;
    }
}
```

While the *Interpreter* pattern does not in itself cover the parsing of an expression, in practice we need to define a class to go through the command string (such as "london edinburgh manchester southerly") and create the appropriate `IExpression` classes as we go along. These `IExpression` classes are placed into a "syntax tree" which is normally implemented using a LIFO[1] stack. We shall therefore define a

---

[1]Last In First Out.

DirectionalEvaluator **class to do this parsing, and set-up a small sample of UK cities:**

```
public class DirectionalEvaluator
{
    private IDictionary<string, City> cities;

    public DirectionalEvaluator()
    {
        cities = new Dictionary<string, City>();

        cities["aberdeen"] = new City("Aberdeen", 57.15, -2.15);
        cities["belfast"] = new City("Belfast", 54.62, -5.93);
        cities["birmingham"] = new City("Birmingham", 52.42, -1.92);
        cities["dublin"] = new City("Dublin", 53.33, -6.25);
        cities["edinburgh"] = new City("Edinburgh", 55.92, -3.02);
        cities["glasgow"] = new City("Glasgow", 55.83, -4.25);
        cities["london"] = new City("London", 51.53, -0.08);
        cities["liverpool"] = new City("Liverpool", 53.42, -3.0);
        cities["manchester"] = new City("Manchester", 53.5, -2.25);
        cities["southampton"] = new City("Southampton", 50.9, -1.38);
    }

    public virtual City Evaluate(string route)
    {
        // Define the syntax tree
        Stack<IExpression> expressionStack
                        = new Stack<IExpression>();

        // Parse each token in route string
        foreach (string token in SplitTokens(route))
        {
            // Is token a recognised city?
            if (cities.ContainsKey(token))
            {
                City city = cities[token];
                expressionStack.Push(new CityExpression(city));

            // Is token to find most northerly?
            }
            else if (token.Equals("northerly"))
            {
                expressionStack.Push(new MostNortherlyExpression
                        (LoadExpressions(expressionStack)));

            // Is token to find most southerly?
            }
            else if (token.Equals("southerly"))
            {
                expressionStack.Push(new MostSoutherlyExpression
                        (LoadExpressions(expressionStack)));

            // Is token to find most westerly?
            }
            else if (token.Equals("westerly"))
            {
```

```
                        expressionStack.Push(new MostWesterlyExpression
                                (LoadExpressions(expressionStack)));

            // Is token to find most easterly?
            }
            else if (token.Equals("easterly"))
            {
                expressionStack.Push(new MostEasterlyExpression
                                (LoadExpressions(expressionStack)));
            }
        }

        // Resulting value
        return expressionStack.Pop().Interpret();
    }

    // Get each separate token from a string
    private IList<string> SplitTokens(string str)
    {
        IList<string> tokens = new List<string>();
        int fromIndex = 0;
        bool finished = false;
        while (!finished)
        {
            int spaceLocation = str.IndexOf(" ", fromIndex);
            if (spaceLocation >= 0)
            {
                tokens.Add(str.Substring(fromIndex,
                            spaceLocation - fromIndex));
                fromIndex = spaceLocation + 1;
            }
            else
            {
                tokens.Add(str.Substring(fromIndex));
                finished = true;
            }
        }
        return tokens;
    }

    private IList<IExpression> LoadExpressions
                (Stack<IExpression> expressionStack)
    {
        IList<IExpression> expressions = new List<IExpression>();
        while (expressionStack.Count > 0)
        {
            expressions.Add(expressionStack.Pop());
        }
        return expressions;
    }
}
```

Within the `Evaluate()` method, when the parser detects a directional command (such as "northerly") it removes the cities on the stack and passes them along with the command back to the stack.

> Note that the use above of `if...else...` statements has been used simply so that the chapter concentrates on the *Interpreter* pattern. A better approach would be to use a separate pattern to handle each token such as that defined in *Chain of Responsibility*.

Now all that remains is for our client programs to utilise the `DirectionalEvaluator` passing the command to interpret:

```
// Create the evaluator
DirectionalEvaluator evaluator = new DirectionalEvaluator();

// This should output "London"...
Console.WriteLine(evaluator.Evaluate
        ("london edinburgh manchester southerly"));

// This should output "Aberdeen"...
Console.WriteLine(evaluator.Evaluate
        ("london edinburgh manchester southerly aberdeen westerly"));

Console.Read();
```

17. Iterator

Type	Behavioural
Purpose	Provide a way to access the elements of an aggregate object sequentially without exposing its underlying representation.

The Foobar Motor Company wanted to produce a brochure listing their range of vehicles for sale and allocated the task to two separate programmers, one to provide the range of cars and the other to provide the range of vans.

The programmer that coded the CarRange class decided to internally store the range using an IList object:

```
public class CarRange
{
    private IList<IVehicle> cars;

    public CarRange()
    {
        cars = new List<IVehicle>();

        // Define the range of car models available
        cars.Add(new Saloon(new StandardEngine(1300)));
        cars.Add(new Saloon(new StandardEngine(1600)));
        cars.Add(new Coupe(new StandardEngine(2000)));
        cars.Add(new Sport(new TurboEngine(2500)));
    }

    public virtual IList<IVehicle> Range
    {
        get
        {
            return cars;
        }
    }

}
```

You can see from the above that the programmer provided a Range getter that returns the IList collection object.

The other programmer decided to store the vans in an array when writing the `VanRange` class, and therefore his version of the `Range` getter returns an array of vehicles:

```
public class VanRange
{
    private IVehicle[] vans;

    public VanRange()
    {
        vans = new IVehicle[3];

        // Define the range of van models available
        vans[0] = new BoxVan(new StandardEngine(1600));
        vans[1] = new BoxVan(new StandardEngine(2000));
        vans[2] = new Pickup(new TurboEngine(2200));
    }

    public virtual IVehicle[] Range
    {
        get
        {
            return vans;
        }
    }
}
```

The problem with this is that the internal representation in both of these classes has been exposed to outside objects.

A better approach would be for each of the `CarRange` and `VanRange` classes to provide a `GetEnumerator()` method that returns an `IEnumerator` object, so that as well as being consistent, the internal representation would not need be exposed.

For `CarRange` the additional method will be as follows:

```
public virtual IEnumerator<IVehicle> GetEnumerator()
{
    return cars.GetEnumerator();
}
```

For `VanRange` the additional method will need to convert from the array:

```
public virtual IEnumerator<IVehicle> GetEnumerator()
{
    return ((IEnumerable<IVehicle>) vans).GetEnumerator();
}
```

Now we can process both cars and vans in a consistent manner:

```
Console.WriteLine("=== Our Cars ===");
CarRange carRange = new CarRange();
PrintIterator(carRange.GetEnumerator());

Console.WriteLine("=== Our Vans ===");
VanRange vanRange = new VanRange();
PrintIterator(vanRange.GetEnumerator());

private static void PrintIterator(IEnumerator iter)
{
    while (iter.MoveNext())
    {
        Console.WriteLine(iter.Current);
    }
}
```

The 'foreach' loop

Several of the other chapters in this book have made use of the `foreach` statement, providing a clean alternative to the above, as follows:

```
Console.WriteLine("=== Our Cars ===");
CarRange carRange = new CarRange();
foreach (IVehicle currentVehicle in carRange.Range) {
    Console.WriteLine(currentVehicle);
}

Console.WriteLine("=== Our Vans ===");
VanRange vanRange = new VanRange();
foreach (IVehicle currentVehicle : vanRange.Range) {
    Console.WriteLine(currentVehicle);
}
```

18. Mediator

Type	Behavioural
Purpose	Define an object that encapsulates how a set of objects interact. *Mediator* promotes loose coupling by keeping objects from referring to each other explicitly, and it lets you vary their interaction independently.

The Foobar Motor Company is looking to the future when vehicles can drive themselves. This, of course, would entail the various components (ignition, gearbox, accelerator and brakes, etc.) being controlled together and interacting in various ways. For example:

• *Until the ignition is switched on, the gearbox, accelerator and brakes do not operate (we will assume the parking brake is in effect);*

• *When accelerating, the brakes should be disabled;*

• *When braking the accelerator should be disabled;*

• *The appropriate gear should be engaged dependent upon the speed of the vehicle.*

And all this should happen automatically so the driver can just enjoy the view! (We will assume the vehicle can sense its position so as to avoid crashes, etc.).

We will naturally create classes to model the individual components, so there will be an `Ignition` class, a `Gearbox` class, an `Accelerator` class and a `Brake` class. But we can also see that there are some complex interactions between them, and yet one of our core object-oriented design principles is to keep classes loosely-coupled.

The *Mediator* pattern helps to solve this through the definition of a separate class (the mediator) that knows about the individual component classes and takes responsibility for managing their interaction. The component classes also each know about the mediator class, but this is the only coupling they have. For our example, we will call the mediator class `EngineManagementSystem`.

We can see the connections diagrammatically below:

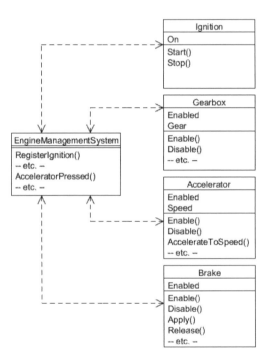

Figure 18.1 : Mediator pattern

The two-way communication is achieved via each of the component classes' constructors, in that they each accept a reference to the mediator object (so they can send messages to it) and register themselves with the mediator (so they can receive messages from it). But each component class has no knowledge of any other component class; they only know about the mediator.

We can see this by looking at the `Ignition` class:

```
public class Ignition
{
    private EngineManagementSystem mediator;
    private bool on;

    // Constructor accepts mediator as an argument
    public Ignition(EngineManagementSystem mediator)
    {
        this.mediator = mediator;
        on = false;

        // Register back with the mediator;
        mediator.RegisterIgnition(this);
    }

    public virtual void Start()
    {
        on = true;
        mediator.IgnitionTurnedOn();
        Console.WriteLine("Ignition turned on");
    }

    public virtual void Stop()
    {
        on = false;
        mediator.IgnitionTurnedOff();
        Console.WriteLine("Ignition turned off");
    }

    public virtual bool On
    {
        get
        {
            return on;
        }
    }
}
```

Note how the constructor establishes the two-way communication, and then how methods that perform events notify the mediator of those events.

The `Gearbox` class applies the same principles:

```
public class Gearbox
{
    private EngineManagementSystem mediator;
    private bool enabled;
    private Gear currentGear;

    // Constructor accepts mediator as an argument
```

```
    public Gearbox(EngineManagementSystem mediator)
    {
        this.mediator = mediator;
        enabled = false;
        currentGear = Gear.Neutral;
        mediator.RegisterGearbox(this);
    }

    public virtual void Enable()
    {
        enabled = true;
        mediator.GearboxEnabled();
        Console.WriteLine("Gearbox enabled");
    }

    public virtual void Disable()
    {
        enabled = false;
        mediator.GearboxDisabled();
        Console.WriteLine("Gearbox disabled");
    }

    public virtual bool Enabled
    {
        get
        {
            return enabled;
        }
    }

    public virtual Gear Gear
    {
        set
        {
            if ((Enabled) && (Gear != value))
            {
                currentGear = value;
                mediator.GearChanged();
                Console.WriteLine("Now in " + Gear + " gear");
            }
        }
        get
        {
            return currentGear;
        }
    }
}
```

The Gear enum used by Gearbox is as follows:

```
public enum Gear
{
    Neutral,
    First,
    Second,
    Third,
```

```
        Fourth,
        Fifth,
        Reverse
}
```

The `Accelerator` and `Brake` **classes follow a similar format:**

```
public class Accelerator
{
    private EngineManagementSystem mediator;
    private bool enabled;
    private int speed;

    // Constructor accepts mediator as an argument
    public Accelerator(EngineManagementSystem mediator)
    {
        this.mediator = mediator;
        enabled = false;
        speed = 0;
        mediator.RegisterAccelerator(this);
    }

    public virtual void Enable()
    {
        enabled = true;
        mediator.AcceleratorEnabled();
        Console.WriteLine("Accelerator enabled");
    }

    public virtual void Disable()
    {
        enabled = false;
        mediator.AcceleratorDisabled();
        Console.WriteLine("Accelerator disabled");
    }

    public virtual bool Enabled
    {
        get
        {
            return enabled;
        }
    }

    public virtual void AccelerateToSpeed(int speed)
    {
        if (Enabled)
        {
            this.speed = speed;
            Console.WriteLine("Speed now " + Speed);
        }
    }

    public virtual int Speed
```

```
        {
            get
            {
                return speed;
            }
        }
    }


    public class Brake
    {
        private EngineManagementSystem mediator;
        private bool enabled;
        private bool applied;

        // Constructor accepts mediator as an argument
        public Brake(EngineManagementSystem mediator)
        {
            this.mediator = mediator;
            enabled = false;
            applied = false;
            mediator.RegisterBrake(this);
        }

        public virtual void Enable()
        {
            enabled = true;
            mediator.BrakeEnabled();
            Console.WriteLine("Brakes enabled");
        }

        public virtual void Disable()
        {
            enabled = false;
            mediator.BrakeDisabled();
            Console.WriteLine("Brakes disabled");
        }

        public virtual bool Enabled
        {
            get
            {
                return enabled;
            }
        }

        public virtual void Apply()
        {
            if (Enabled)
            {
                applied = true;
                mediator.BrakePressed();
                Console.WriteLine("Now braking");
            }
        }

        private void Release()
```

```
    {
        if (Enabled)
        {
            applied = false;
        }
    }
}
```

So we now need the `EngineManagementSystem` class to serve as the mediator. This will hold a reference to each of the component classes with methods enabling their registration with the mediator. It also has methods to handle the interaction between the various components when particular events occur:

```
public class EngineManagementSystem
{
    private Ignition ignition;
    private Gearbox gearbox;
    private Accelerator accelerator;
    private Brake brake;

    private int currentSpeed;

    public EngineManagementSystem()
    {
        currentSpeed = 0;
    }


    // Methods that enable registration with this mediator...

    public virtual void RegisterIgnition(Ignition ignition)
    {
        this.ignition = ignition;
    }

    public virtual void RegisterGearbox(Gearbox gearbox)
    {
        this.gearbox = gearbox;
    }

    public virtual void RegisterAccelerator(Accelerator accelerator)
    {
        this.accelerator = accelerator;
    }

    public virtual void RegisterBrake(Brake brake)
    {
        this.brake = brake;
    }
```

```csharp
// Methods that handle object interactions...

public virtual void IgnitionTurnedOn()
{
    gearbox.Enable();
    accelerator.Enable();
    brake.Enable();
}

public virtual void IgnitionTurnedOff()
{
    gearbox.Disable();
    accelerator.Disable();
    brake.Disable();
}

public virtual void GearboxEnabled()
{
    Console.WriteLine("EMS now controlling the gearbox");
}

public virtual void GearboxDisabled()
{
    Console.WriteLine("EMS no longer controlling the gearbox");
}

public virtual void GearChanged()
{
    Console.WriteLine("EMS disengaging revs while gear changing");
}

public virtual void AcceleratorEnabled()
{
    Console.WriteLine("EMS now controlling the accelerator");
}

public virtual void AcceleratorDisabled()
{
    Console.WriteLine("EMS no longer controlling the accelerator");
}

public virtual void AcceleratorPressed()
{
    brake.Disable();
    while (currentSpeed < accelerator.Speed)
    {
        currentSpeed++;
        Console.WriteLine("Speed currentlt " + currentSpeed);
        // Set gear according to speed
        if (currentSpeed <= 10)
        {
            gearbox.Gear = Gear.First;
        }
        else if (currentSpeed <= 20)
        {
            gearbox.Gear = Gear.Second;
        }
```

```
            else if (currentSpeed <= 30)
            {
                gearbox.Gear = Gear.Third;
            }
            else if (currentSpeed <= 50)
            {
                gearbox.Gear = Gear.Fourth;
            }
            else
            {
                gearbox.Gear = Gear.Fifth;
            }
        }
        brake.Enable();
    }

    public virtual void BrakeEnabled()
    {
        Console.WriteLine("EMS now controlling the brake");
    }

    public virtual void BrakeDisabled()
    {
        Console.WriteLine("EMS no longer controlling the brake");
    }

    public virtual void BrakePressed()
    {
        accelerator.Disable();
        currentSpeed = 0;
    }

    public virtual void BrakeReleased()
    {
        gearbox.Gear = Gear.First;
        accelerator.Enable();
    }
}
```

Common uses

A common use of the *Mediator* pattern is to manage the interaction of graphical components on a dialog. This frequently involves controlling when buttons, text fields, etc. should be enabled or disabled, or for passing data between components.

Note that it may be possible to reduce coupling further by using the *Observer* pattern in place of *Mediator*. This would mean that the component classes (i.e. Ignition, etc.) would not need to hold a reference to a mediator but would instead fire events. The `EngineManagementSystem` class would then be an observer of the component classes and would still be able to invoke messages on them.

19. Memento

Type	Behavioural
Purpose	Without violating encapsulation, capture and externalise an object's internal state so that it can be restored to this state later.

The Foobar Motor Company's vehicles naturally have a speedometer mounted on the dashboard, which not only records the current speed but also the previous speed. There is now a requirement for the state to be stored externally at periodic intervals (so that it could, for example, be integrated into a tachograph for goods vehicles).

However, the previous speed instance variable in the Speedometer class does not have a getter method. We also want to adhere to the principle that a class should not have multiple responsibilities, so don't want to also have to build in a state save & restore mechanism into the class. So how can we capture the state of the object?

This chapter will present two different approaches, each having its advantages and disadvantages. In both cases, we make use of a separate class that performs the state saving and restoration, which we shall call SpeedometerMemento. This class takes a reference to the Speedometer object that needs to be externalised:

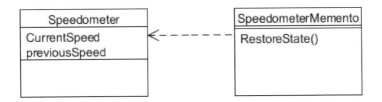

Figure 19.1 : Memento pattern

Approach 1 – using internal visibility

When the access modifier `internal` is specified this means the member is only accessible to other classes in the same assembly. Therefore we can place the `Speedometer` class and its associated memento class into their own assembly, and we will call the latter class `SpeedometerMemento`.

Here is the very simple `Speedometer` class:

```
namespace AssemblyNamespace
{
    public class Speedometer
    {
        // Normal private visibility but has getter method...
        private int currentSpeed;

        // internal visibility and no getter method...
        internal int previousSpeed;

        public Speedometer()
        {
            currentSpeed = 0;
            previousSpeed = 0;
        }

        public virtual int CurrentSpeed
        {
            set
            {
                previousSpeed = currentSpeed;
                currentSpeed = value;
            }
            get
            {
                return currentSpeed;
            }
        }
    }
}
```

The `SpeedometerMemento` class exists in the same assembly. It saves the state of the passed in `Speedometer` object in the constructor and defines a method to restore that state:

```
namespace AssemblyNamespace
{
    public class SpeedometerMemento
    {
        private Speedometer speedometer;
```

```
        private int copyOfCurrentSpeed;
        private int copyOfPreviousSpeed;

        public SpeedometerMemento(Speedometer speedometer)
        {
            this.speedometer = speedometer;
            copyOfCurrentSpeed = speedometer.CurrentSpeed;
            copyOfPreviousSpeed = speedometer.previousSpeed;
        }

        public virtual void RestoreState()
        {
            speedometer.CurrentSpeed = copyOfCurrentSpeed;
            speedometer.previousSpeed = copyOfPreviousSpeed;
        }
    }
}
```

Note that the CurrentSpeed property getter was used for the currentSpeed instance variable but the previousSpeed variable had to be accessed directly, which is possible because the memento exists in the same assembly.

We can test the memento with this code:

```
Speedometer speedo = new Speedometer();

speedo.CurrentSpeed = 50;
speedo.CurrentSpeed = 100;
Console.WriteLine("Current speed: " + speedo.CurrentSpeed);
Console.WriteLine("Previous speed: " + speedo.previousSpeed);

// Save the state of 'speedo'
SpeedometerMemento memento = new SpeedometerMemento(speedo);

// Change the state of 'speedo'
speedo.CurrentSpeed = 80;
Console.WriteLine("After setting to 80...");
Console.WriteLine("Current speed: " + speedo.CurrentSpeed);
Console.WriteLine("Previous speed: " + speedo.previousSpeed);

// Restore the state of 'speedo'
Console.WriteLine("Now restoring state...");
memento.RestoreState();
Console.WriteLine("Current speed: " + speedo.CurrentSpeed);
Console.WriteLine("Previous speed: " + speedo.previousSpeed);

Console.Read();
```

Running the above results in the following output:

```
Current speed: 100
Previous speed: 50

After setting to 80...
Current speed: 80
Previous speed: 100

Now restoring state...
Current speed: 100
Previous speed: 50
```

The main disadvantage of this approach is that you either have to put the pair of classes in their own separate assembly or accept that other classes in the assembly they are in will have direct access to the instance variables.

Approach 2 – object serialization

This approach allows you to make all the instance variables `private`, thus regaining full encapsulation. The `Speedometer` class has been modified for this and now includes a `PreviousSpeed` getter, though this is purely to help us test the memento; it's not required by this approach. The class has also been changed be `Serializable` (changes marked in bold):

```
[Serializable]
public class Speedometer
{
    private int currentSpeed;
    private int previousSpeed;

    public Speedometer2() {
        currentSpeed = 0;
        previousSpeed = 0;
    }

    public virtual int CurrentSpeed {
        set {
            previousSpeed = currentSpeed;
            currentSpeed = value;
        }
        Get
```

```
        {
            return currentSpeed;
        }
    }

    // Only defined to help testing...
    public virtual int PreviousSpeed {
        get
        {
            return previousSpeed;
        }
    }
}
```

The `SpeedometerMemento` class now uses object serialization for the state saving and restoration:

```
public class SpeedometerMemento
{
    public SpeedometerMemento(Speedometer speedometer)
    {
        // Serialize...
        Stream stream = File.Open("speedometer.ser", FileMode.Create);
        BinaryFormatter formatter = new BinaryFormatter();
        formatter.Serialize(stream, speedometer);
        stream.Close();
    }

    public virtual Speedometer RestoreState()
    {
        // Deserialize...
        Speedometer2 speedo;
        Stream stream = File.Open("speedometer.ser", FileMode.Open);
        BinaryFormatter formatter = new BinaryFormatter();
        speedo = (Speedometer)formatter.Deserialize(stream);
        stream.Close();
        return speedo;
    }

}
```

We can check that this achieves the same as the first approach, the only difference being that the `RestoreState()` method now returns the restored object reference:

```
Speedometer speedo = new Speedometer();

speedo.CurrentSpeed = 50;
speedo.CurrentSpeed = 100;
Console.WriteLine("Current speed: " + speedo.CurrentSpeed);
```

```
Console.WriteLine("Previous speed: " + speedo.PreviousSpeed);

// Save the state of 'speedo'
SpeedometerMemento memento = new SpeedometerMemento(speedo);

// Change the state of 'speedo'
speedo.CurrentSpeed = 80;
Console.WriteLine("After setting to 80...");
Console.WriteLine("Current speed: " + speedo.CurrentSpeed);
Console.WriteLine("Previous speed: " + speedo.PreviousSpeed);

// Restore the state of 'speedo'
Console.WriteLine("Now restoring state...");
speedo = memento.RestoreState();
Console.WriteLine("Current speed: " + speedo.CurrentSpeed);
Console.WriteLine("Previous speed: " + speedo.PreviousSpeed);
Console.Read();
```

Running the above should result in the same output as shown for the first approach. The main disadvantage of this approach is that writing to and reading from a disk file is much slower. Note also that while we have been able to make all fields `private` again, it might still be possible for someone who gained access to the serialized file to use a hex editor to read or change the data.

20. Observer

Type	Behavioural
Purpose	Define a one-to-many dependency between objects so that when one object changes its state, all its dependants are notified and updated automatically.

The Foobar Motor Company has decided that an alert should sound to the driver whenever a certain speed is exceeded. They also envisage that other things may need to happen depending upon the current speed (such as an automatic gearbox selecting the appropriate gear to match the speed). But they realise the need to keep objects loosely-coupled, so naturally don't wish the Speedometer class to have any direct knowledge of speed monitors or automatic gearboxes (or any other future class that might be interested in the speed a vehicle is travelling).

The *Observer* pattern enables a loose-coupling to be established between a 'subject' (the object that is of interest; Speedometer in our example) and its 'observers' (any other class that needs to be kept informed when interesting stuff happens).

Because this is a very common need in object-oriented systems, the C# libraries already contains mechanisms that enable the pattern to be implemented. One of these is by utilising the EventHandler event class.

The 'subject' (Speedometer) can have multiple observers, each of which will be notified whenever an event occurs on the Speedometer object. The Speedometer class looks like this[1]:

```
public class Speedometer
{
    public event EventHandler ValueChanged;
    private int currentSpeed;

    public Speedometer()
```

[1] Unlike the version in the *Memento* pattern chapter, there is no variable to record the previous speed as it is irrelevant to this example.

```
        {
            speed = 0;
        }

        public virtual int CurrentSpeed
        {
            set
            {
                currentSpeed = value;

                // Tell all observers so they know value has changed...
                OnValueChanged();
            }
            get
            {
                return currentSpeed;
            }
        }

        protected void OnValueChanged()
        {
            if (ValueChanged != null)
            {
                ValueChanged(this, EventArgs.Empty);
            }
        }
    }
}
```

The `SpeedMonitor` **utilises** `ValueChanged`:

```
    public class SpeedMonitor
    {
        public const int SpeedToAlert = 70;

        public SpeedMonitor(Speedometer speedo)
        {
            speedo.ValueChanged += ValueHasChanged;
        }

        private void ValueHasChanged(object sender, EventArgs e )
        {
            Speedometer speedo = (Speedometer)sender;
            if (speedo.CurrentSpeed > SpeedToAlert)
            {
                Console.WriteLine("** ALERT ** Driving too fast! ("
                                + speedo.CurrentSpeed + ")");
            }
            else
            {
                Console.WriteLine("... nice and steady ... ("
                                + speedo.CurrentSpeed + ")");
            }
        }
    }
}
```

Client programs simply pass a `SpeedMonitor` reference to an instance of `Speedometer`:

```
// Create a speedometer...
Speedometer speedo = new Speedometer();

// Create a monitor...
SpeedMonitor monitor = new SpeedMonitor(speedo);

// Drive at different speeds...
speedo.CurrentSpeed = 50;
speedo.CurrentSpeed = 70;
speedo.CurrentSpeed = 40;
speedo.CurrentSpeed = 100;
speedo.CurrentSpeed = 69;

Console.Read();
```

Running the above will result in the following output:

```
... nice and steady ... (50)
... nice and steady ... (70)
... nice and steady ... (40)
** ALERT ** Driving too fast! (100)
... nice and steady ... (69)
```

The real power behind the *Observer* pattern is that any type of class can now become a monitor without requiring any changes to be made to `Speedometer`. Let's create a simulation of an automatic gearbox:

```
public class AutomaticGearbox
{
    public AutomaticGearbox(Speedometer speedo)
    {
        speedo.ValueChanged += ValueHasChanged;
    }

    private void ValueHasChanged(object sender, EventArgs e )
    {
        Speedometer speedo = (Speedometer)sender;
        if (speedo.CurrentSpeed <= 10)
        {
            Console.WriteLine("Now in first gear");

        }
        else if (speedo.CurrentSpeed <= 20)
        {
```

```
            Console.WriteLine("Now in second gear");
        }
        else if (speedo.CurrentSpeed <= 30)
        {
            Console.WriteLine("Now in third gear");
        }
        else
        {
            Console.WriteLine("Now in fourth gear");
        }
    }
}
```

Our client program can now just add this as an additional observer and get notifications of speed changes as well:

```
AutomaticGearbox auto = new AutomaticGearbox(speedo);
```

21. State

Type	Behavioural
Purpose	Allow an object to alter its behaviour when its internal state changes. The object will appear to change its class.

The Foobar Motor Company's vehicles each have a digital clock fitted that displays the current date and time. These values will need to be reset from time to time (such as after a change of battery) and this is accomplished by means of a particular knob on the dashboard. When the knob is initially pressed, the 'year' value can be set. Turning the knob to the left (i.e. anti-clockwise) causes the previous year to be show, whereas turning it to the right goes forward one year. When the knob is pressed again the year value becomes 'set' and the set-up process then automatically allows the month value to be set, also by making appropriate left or right movements with the knob.

This process continues for the day of the month, the hour and the minute. The following table summarises the flow of events:

User Action	What Happens
Push knob	Clock goes into 'setup' mode for setting **year**
Rotate knob left	1 is deducted from the **year** value
Rotate knob right	1 is added to the **year** value
Push knob	Year now set and automatically transitions into **month** set-up
Rotate knob left	1 is deducted from the **month** value
Rotate knob right	1 is added to the **month** value
Push knob	Month now set and automatically transitions into **day** set-up
Rotate knob left	1 is deducted from the **day** value
Rotate knob right	1 is added to the **day** value

Push knob	Day now set and automatically transitions into **hour** set-up
Rotate knob left	1 is deducted from the **hour** value
Rotate knob right	1 is added to the **hour** value
Push knob	Hour now set and automatically transitions into **minute** set-up
Rotate knob left	1 is deducted from the **minute** value
Rotate knob right	1 is added to the **minute** value
Push knob	Minute now set and automatically transitions for into 'finished' mode
Push knob	Displays set date & time

From the above steps it is clear that different parts of the date & time get set when the knob is turned or pressed, and that there are transitions between those parts. A naive approach when coding a class to accomplish this would be to have a 'mode' variable and then a series of if...else... statements in each method, which might look like this:

```
// *** DON'T DO THIS! ***
public void RotateKnobLeft()
{
    if (mode == YearMode)
    {
        year--;
    }
    else if (mode == MonthMode)
    {
        month--;
    }
    else if (mode == DayMode)
    {
        day--;
    }
    else if (mode == HourMode)
    {
        hour--;
    }
    else if (mode == MinuteMode)
    {
        minute--;
    }
}
```

The problem with code such as the above is that the `if...else...` conditions would have to be repeated in each action method (i.e. `RotateKnobRight()`, `PushKnob()`, etc.). Apart from making the code look unwieldy it also becomes hard to maintain, as if for example we now need to record seconds we would need to change multiple parts of the class.

The *State* pattern enables a hierarchy to be established that allows for state transitions such as necessitated by our clock setting example. We will create a `ClockSetup` class that initiates the states through the interface `IClockSetupState`, which has an implementing class for each individual state:

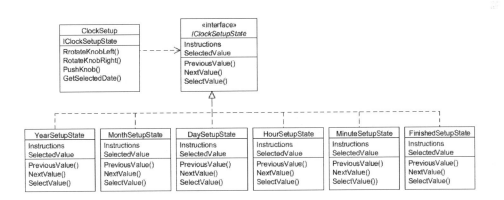

Figure 21.1 : State pattern

The `IClockSetupState` interface defines methods for handling changes to the state, plus methods that can provide user instructions and return the actual selected value:

```
public interface IClockSetupState
{
    void PreviousValue();
    void NextValue();
    void SelectValue();

    string Instructions { get; }
    int SelectedValue { get; }
}
```

Looking first at `YearSetupState`, you will notice that it takes a reference to a `ClockSetup` object (to be defined later) in the constructor (which is known in the language of design patterns as its 'context') and manages the setting of the year. Note in particular in the `SelectValue()` method how it transitions internally to a different state:

```
public class YearSetupState : IClockSetupState
{
    private ClockSetup clockSetup;
    private int year;

    public YearSetupState(ClockSetup clockSetup)
    {
        this.clockSetup = clockSetup;
        year = DateTime.Now.Year;
    }

    public virtual void PreviousValue()
    {
        year--;
    }

    public virtual void NextValue()
    {
        year++;
    }

    public virtual void SelectValue()
    {
        Console.WriteLine("Year set to " + year);
        clockSetup.State = clockSetup.MonthSetupState;
    }

    public virtual string Instructions
    {
        get
        {
            return "Please set the year...";
        }
    }

    public virtual int SelectedValue
    {
        get
        {
            return year;
        }
    }
}
```

The other date & time state classes follow a similar process, each transitioning to the next appropriate state when required:

```
public class MonthSetupState : IClockSetupState
{
    private ClockSetup clockSetup;
    private int month;

    public MonthSetupState(ClockSetup clockSetup)
    {
        this.clockSetup = clockSetup;
        month = DateTime.Now.Month;
    }

    public virtual void PreviousValue()
    {
        if (month > 1)
        {
            month--;
        }
    }

    public virtual void NextValue()
    {
        if (month < 12)
        {
            month++;
        }
    }

    public virtual void SelectValue()
    {
        Console.WriteLine("Month set to " + month);
        clockSetup.State = clockSetup.DaySetupState;
    }

    public virtual string Instructions
    {
        get
        {
            return "Please set the month...";
        }
    }

    public virtual int SelectedValue
    {
        get
        {
            return month;
        }
    }
}


public class DaySetupState : IClockSetupState
```

```
    {
        private ClockSetup clockSetup;
        private int day;

        public DaySetupState(ClockSetup clockSetup)
        {
            this.clockSetup = clockSetup;
            day = DateTime.Now.Day;
        }

        public virtual void PreviousValue()
        {
            if (day > 1)
            {
                day--;
            }
        }

        public virtual void NextValue()
        {
            if (day < System.DateTime.DaysInMonth(new DateTime().Year,
                                            new DateTime().Month))
            {
                day++;
            }
        }

        public virtual void SelectValue()
        {
            Console.WriteLine("Day set to " + day);
            clockSetup.State = clockSetup.HourSetupState;
        }

        public virtual string Instructions
        {
            get
            {
                return "Please set the day...";
            }
        }

        public virtual int SelectedValue
        {
            get
            {
                return day;
            }
        }
    }



    public class HourSetupState : IClockSetupState
    {
        private ClockSetup clockSetup;
        private int hour;
```

```
    public HourSetupState(ClockSetup clockSetup)
    {
        this.clockSetup = clockSetup;
        hour = DateTime.Now.Hour;
    }

    public virtual void PreviousValue()
    {
        if (hour > 0)
        {
            hour--;
        }
    }

    public virtual void NextValue()
    {
        if (hour < 23)
        {
            hour++;
        }
    }

    public virtual void SelectValue()
    {
        Console.WriteLine("Hour set to " + hour);
        clockSetup.State = clockSetup.MinuteSetupState;
    }

    public virtual string Instructions
    {
        get
        {
            return "Please set the hour...";
        }
    }

    public virtual int SelectedValue
    {
        get
        {
            return hour;
        }
    }
}


public class MinuteSetupState : IClockSetupState
{
    private ClockSetup clockSetup;
    private int minute;

    public MinuteSetupState(ClockSetup clockSetup)
    {
        this.clockSetup = clockSetup;
        minute = DateTime.Now.Minute;
    }
```

```
    public virtual void PreviousValue()
    {
        if (minute > 0)
        {
            minute--;
        }
    }

    public virtual void NextValue()
    {
        if (minute < 59)
        {
            minute++;
        }
    }

    public virtual void SelectValue()
    {
        Console.WriteLine("Minute set to " + minute);
        clockSetup.State = clockSetup.FinishedSetupState;
    }

    public virtual string Instructions
    {
        get
        {
            return "Please set the minute...";
        }
    }

    public virtual int SelectedValue
    {
        get
        {
            return minute;
        }
    }
}
```

This just leaves the FinishedSetupState class which doesn't need to transition to a different state:

```
public class FinishedSetupState : IClockSetupState
{
    private ClockSetup clockSetup;

    public FinishedSetupState(ClockSetup clockSetup)
    {
        this.clockSetup = clockSetup;
    }

    public virtual void PreviousValue()
    {
```

```
            Console.WriteLine("Ignored...");
        }

        public virtual void NextValue()
        {
            Console.WriteLine("Ignored...");
        }

        public virtual void SelectValue()
        {
            DateTime selectedDate = clockSetup.SelectedDate;
            Console.WriteLine("Date set to: " + selectedDate);
        }

        public virtual string Instructions
        {
            get
            {
                return "Press knob to view selected date...";
            }
        }

        public virtual int SelectedValue
        {
            get
            {
                throw new System.NotSupportedException
                                ("Clock setup finished");
            }
        }
    }
}
```

As mentioned, the 'context' class is `ClockSetup`, which holds references to each state and forwards to whichever is the current state:

```
public class ClockSetup
{
    // The various states the setup can be in...
    private IClockSetupState yearState;
    private IClockSetupState monthState;
    private IClockSetupState dayState;
    private IClockSetupState hourState;
    private IClockSetupState minuteState;
    private IClockSetupState finishedState;

    // The current state we are in...
    private IClockSetupState currentState;

    public ClockSetup()
    {
        yearState = new YearSetupState(this);
        monthState = new MonthSetupState(this);
        dayState = new DaySetupState(this);
        hourState = new HourSetupState(this);
```

```
        minuteState = new MinuteSetupState(this);
        finishedState = new FinishedSetupState(this);

        // Initial state is set to the year
        State = yearState;
    }

    public virtual IClockSetupState State
    {
        set
        {
            currentState = value;
            Console.WriteLine(currentState.Instructions);
        }
    }

    public virtual void RotateKnobLeft()
    {
        currentState.PreviousValue();
    }

    public virtual void RotateKnobRight()
    {
        currentState.NextValue();
    }

    public virtual void PushKnob()
    {
        currentState.SelectValue();
    }

    public virtual IClockSetupState YearSetupState
    {
        get
        {
            return yearState;
        }
    }

    public virtual IClockSetupState MonthSetupState
    {
        get
        {
            return monthState;
        }
    }

    public virtual IClockSetupState DaySetupState
    {
        get
        {
            return dayState;
        }
    }

    public virtual IClockSetupState HourSetupState
    {
```

```
        get
        {
            return hourState;
        }
    }

    public virtual IClockSetupState MinuteSetupState
    {
        get
        {
            return minuteState;
        }
    }

    public virtual IClockSetupState FinishedSetupState
    {
        get
        {
            return finishedState;
        }
    }

    public virtual DateTime SelectedDate
    {
        get
        {
            return new DateTime(yearState.SelectedValue,
                                monthState.SelectedValue,
                                dayState.SelectedValue,
                                hourState.SelectedValue,
                                minuteState.SelectedValue,
                                0);
        }
    }
}
```

1

We can simulate a user's example actions like this:

```
ClockSetup clockSetup = new ClockSetup();

// Setup starts in 'year' state
clockSetup.RotateKnobRight();
clockSetup.PushKnob(); // year should be 1 on from current

// Setup should now be in 'month' state
clockSetup.RotateKnobRight();
clockSetup.RotateKnobRight();
clockSetup.PushKnob(); // month should be 2 on from current

// Setup should now be in 'day' state
clockSetup.RotateKnobRight();
clockSetup.RotateKnobRight();
clockSetup.RotateKnobRight();
clockSetup.PushKnob(); // day should be 3 on from current
```

```
// Setup should now be in 'hour' state
clockSetup.RotateKnobLeft();
clockSetup.RotateKnobLeft();
clockSetup.PushKnob(); // hour should be 2 less than current

// Setup should now be in 'minute' state
clockSetup.RotateKnobRight();
clockSetup.PushKnob(); // minute should be 1 on than current

// Setup should now be in 'finished' state
clockSetup.PushKnob(); // to display selected date

Console.Read();
```

Running the above should result in the following output should give output relative to your current system date, time and locale format, with the above adjustments made.

```
Please set the year...
Year set to 2013
Please set the month...
Month set to 11
Please set the day...
Day set to 25
Please set the hour...
Hour set to 9
Please set the minute...
Minute set to 17
Press knob to view selected date...
Date set to: 25/11/2013 09:17:00
```

22. Strategy

Type	Behavioural
Purpose	Define a family of algorithms, encapsulate each one, and make them interchangeable. *Strategy* lets the algorithm vary independently from clients that use it.

The Foobar Motor Company wishes to implement a new type of automatic gearbox for their cars that will be able to be switched between its standard mode and a special 'sport' mode. The different modes will base the decision of which gear should be selected depending upon the speed of travel, size of the engine and whether it is turbocharged. And it's quite possible they will want other modes in the future, such as for off-road driving.

Just as with the discussion in the chapter for the *State* pattern, it would be inflexible to use a series of if...else... statements to control the different gearbox modes directly inside our vehicle classes. Instead, we shall encapsulate the concept that varies and define a separate hierarchy so that each different gearbox mode is a separate class, each in effect being a different 'strategy' that gets applied. This approach allows the actual strategy being used to be isolated from the vehicle. In our example, we shall only apply this to the cars:

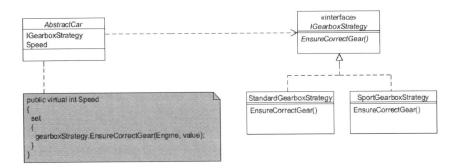

Figure 22.1 : Strategy pattern

The `IGearboxStrategy` **interface defines the method to control the gear:**

```
public interface IGearboxStrategy
{
    void EnsureCorrectGear(IEngine engine, int speed);
}
```

There are two implementing classes; `StandardGearboxStrategy` **and** `SportGearboxStrategy`**:**

```
public class StandardGearboxStrategy : IGearboxStrategy
{
    public virtual void EnsureCorrectGear(IEngine engine, int speed)
    {
        int engineSize = engine.Size;
        bool turbo = engine.Turbo;

        // Some complicated code to determine correct gear
        // setting based on engineSize, turbo & speed, etc.
        // ... omitted ...
        Console.WriteLine("Working out correct gear at "
                    + speed + "mph for a STANDARD gearbox");
    }
}
```

```
public class SportGearboxStrategy : IGearboxStrategy
{
    public virtual void EnsureCorrectGear(IEngine engine, int speed)
    {
        int engineSize = engine.Size;
        bool turbo = engine.Turbo;

        // Some complicated code to determine correct gear
        // setting based on engineSize, turbo & speed, etc.
        // ... omitted ...

        Console.WriteLine("Working out correct gear at "
                    + speed + "mph for a SPORT gearbox");
    }
}
```

Our `AbstractCar` **class is defined to hold a reference to the interface type (i.e.** `IGearboxStrategy`**) and provide accessors so that different strategies can be switched. There is also a** `Speed` **property setter that delegates to whatever strategy is in effect. The pertinent code is marked in bold:**

```
public abstract class AbstractCar : AbstractVehicle
```

```
{
    private IGearboxStrategy gearboxStrategy;

    public AbstractCar(IEngine engine)
            : this(engine, VehicleColour.Unpainted)
    {
    }

    public AbstractCar(IEngine engine, VehicleColour colour)
            : base(engine, colour)
    {
        // Starts in standard gearbox mode (more economical)
        gearboxStrategy = new StandardGearboxStrategy();
    }

    // Allow the gearbox strategy to be changed...
    public virtual IGearboxStrategy IGearboxStrategy
    {
        set
        {
            gearboxStrategy = value;
        }
        get
        {
            return gearboxStrategy;
        }
    }

    public virtual int Speed
    {
        set
        {
            // Delegate to strategy in effect...
            gearboxStrategy.EnsureCorrectGear(Engine, value);
        }
    }
}
```

Client programs just set the required strategy:

```
AbstractCar myCar = new Sport(new StandardEngine(2000));
myCar.Speed = 20;
myCar.Speed = 40;

Console.WriteLine("Switching on sports mode gearbox...");
myCar.IGearboxStrategy = new SportGearboxStrategy();
myCar.Speed = 20;
myCar.Speed = 40;

Console.Read();
```

This should result in the following output:

```
Working out correct gear at 20mph for a STANDARD gearbox
Working out correct gear at 40mph for a STANDARD gearbox
Switching on sports mode gearbox...
Working out correct gear at 20mph for a SPORT gearbox
Working out correct gear at 40mph for a SPORT gearbox
```

23. Template Method

Type	Behavioural
Purpose	Define the skeleton of an algorithm in a method, deferring some steps to subclasses. *Template Method* lets subclasses redefine certain steps of an algorithm without changing the algorithm's structure.

Each vehicle made by the Foobar Motor Company needs a small number of printed booklets to be produced and provided to the buyer, such as an Owner's Manual and a Service History booklet. The way booklets are produced always follows the same set of steps, but each different type of booklet might need to do each of the individual steps in a slightly different way.

The *Template Method* pattern enables the definition of one or more abstract methods that are called through a 'template method'. The simple hierarchy is as follows:

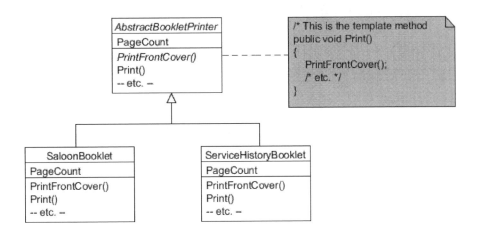

Figure 23.1 : Template Method pattern

The `AbstractBookletPrinter` **class defines several** `protected abstract` **methods and one** `public` 'template method' **that makes use of the abstract methods:**

```
public abstract class AbstractBookletPrinter
{
    protected internal abstract int PageCount { get; }
    protected internal abstract void PrintFrontCover();
    protected internal abstract void PrintTableOfContents();
    protected internal abstract void PrintPage(int pageNumber);
    protected internal abstract void PrintIndex();
    protected internal abstract void PrintBackCover();

    // This is the 'template method'
    public void Print()
    {
        PrintFrontCover();
        PrintTableOfContents();
        for (int i = 1; i <= PageCount; i++)
        {
            PrintPage(i);
        }
        PrintIndex();
        PrintBackCover();
    }
}
```

Each concrete subclass now only needs to provide the implementing code for each abstract method, for example the `SaloonBooklet` class below:

```
public class SaloonBooklet : AbstractBookletPrinter
{
    protected internal override int PageCount
    {
        get
        {
            return 100;
        }
    }

    protected internal override void PrintFrontCover()
    {
        Console.WriteLine
            ("Printing front cover for Saloon car booklet");
    }

    protected internal override void PrintTableOfContents()
    {
        Console.WriteLine
            ("Printing table of contents for Saloon car booklet");
    }
```

```
    protected internal override void PrintPage(int pageNumber)
    {
        Console.WriteLine
       ("Printing page " + pageNumber + " for Saloon car booklet");
    }

    protected internal override void PrintIndex()
    {
        Console.WriteLine("Printing index for Saloon car booklet");
    }

    protected internal override void PrintBackCover()
    {
        Console.WriteLine
            ("Printing back cover for Saloon car booklet");
    }
}
```

The `ServiceHistoryBooklet` **is very similar:**

```
public class ServiceHistoryBooklet : AbstractBookletPrinter
{
    protected internal override int PageCount
    {
        get
        {
            return 12;
        }
    }

    protected internal override void PrintFrontCover()
    {
        Console.WriteLine
          ("Printing front cover for service history booklet");
    }

    protected internal override void PrintTableOfContents()
    {
        Console.WriteLine
       ("Printing table of contents for service history booklet");
    }

    protected internal override void PrintPage(int pageNumber)
    {
            Console.WriteLine
       ("Printing page " + pageNumber + " for service history
       booklet");
    }

    protected internal override void PrintIndex()
    {
        Console.WriteLine
          ("Printing index for service history booklet");
    }
```

```
    protected internal override void PrintBackCover()
    {
        Console.WriteLine
          ("Printing back cover for service history booklet");
    }
}
```

While it is not essential from the point of view of the pattern for the abstract methods to be `protected`, it is often the case that this is the most appropriate access level to assign since they are only intended for over-riding and not for direct invocation by client objects.

Also note that it's perfectly acceptable for some of the methods called from the 'template method' to not be abstract but have a default implementation provided. But when at least one abstract method is being called, it qualifies as the *Template Method* pattern.

Client programs merely need to instantiate the required concrete class and invoke the `Print()` method:

```
Console.WriteLine("About to print a booklet for saloon cars");
AbstractBookletPrinter saloonBooklet = new SaloonBooklet();
saloonBooklet.Print();

Console.WriteLine("About to print a service history booklet");
AbstractBookletPrinter serviceBooklet = new ServiceHistoryBooklet();
serviceBooklet.Print();

Console.Read();
```

24. Visitor

Type	Behavioural
Purpose	Represent a method to be performed on the elements of an object structure. *Visitor* lets you define a new method without changing the classes of the elements on which it operates.

Sometimes a class hierarchy and its code become substantive, and yet it is known that future requirements will be inevitable. An example for the Foobar Motor Company is the IEngine hierarchy which looks like this:

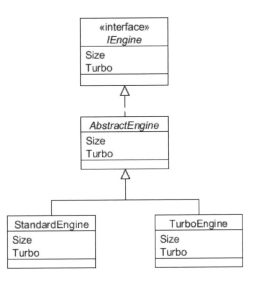

Figure 24.1 : IEngine class hierarchy

In reality, the code within the AbstractEngine class is likely to be composed of a multitude of individual components, such as a camshaft, piston, some spark plugs, etc. If we need to add some functionality that traverses these components then the natural way is to just add a method to AbstractEngine. But maybe we know there are potentially many such new requirements and we would rather not have to keep adding methods directly into the hierarchy?

The *Visitor* pattern enables us to define just one additional method to add into the class hierarchy in such a way that lots of different types of new functionality can be added without any further changes. This is accomplished by means of a technique known as "double-despatch", whereby the invoked method issues a call-back to the invoking object.

The technique requires first the definition of an interface we shall call IEngineVisitor:

```
public interface IEngineVisitor
{
    void Visit(Camshaft camshaft);
    void Visit(IEngine engine);
    void Visit(Piston piston);
    void Visit(SparkPlug sparkPlug);
}
```

We will also define an interface called IVisitable with an AcceptEngineVisitor() method:

```
public interface IVisitable
{
    void AcceptEngineVisitor(IEngineVisitor visitor);
}
```

The IEngine interface you have met in previous chapters (although we will modify it slightly for this chapter). The Camshaft, Piston and SparkPlug classes are each very simple, as follows:

```
public class Camshaft : IVisitable
{
    public virtual void AcceptEngineVisitor(IEngineVisitor visitor)
    {
        visitor.Visit(this);
    }
}


public class Piston : IVisitable
{
    public virtual void AcceptEngineVisitor(IEngineVisitor visitor)
```

```
        {
            visitor.Visit(this);
        }
    }


    public class SparkPlug : IVisitable
    {
        public virtual void AcceptEngineVisitor(IEngineVisitor visitor)
        {
            visitor.Visit(this);
        }
    }
```

As you can see, each of these classes defines a method called AcceptEngineVisitor() that takes a reference to an IEngineVisitor object as its argument. All the method does is invoke the Visit() method of the passed-in IEngineVisitor, passing back the object instance.

Our modified IEngine interface also now extends IVisitable:

```
    public interface IEngine : IVisitable
    {
        int Size { get; }
        bool Turbo { get; }
    }
```

The AbstractEngine class therefore needs to implement this new method, which in this case traverses the individual components (camshaft, piston, spark plugs) invoking AcceptEngineVisitor() on each:

```
    public abstract class AbstractEngine : IEngine
    {
        private int size;
        private bool turbo;

        private Camshaft camshaft;
        private Piston piston;
        private SparkPlug[] sparkPlugs;

        public AbstractEngine(int size, bool turbo)
        {
            this.size = size;
            this.turbo = turbo;

            // Create a camshaft, piston and 4 spark plugs...
            camshaft = new Camshaft();
```

```
            piston = new Piston();
            sparkPlugs = new SparkPlug[]
                        {
                            new SparkPlug(), new SparkPlug(),
                            new SparkPlug(), new SparkPlug()
                        };
    }

    public virtual int Size
    {
        get
        {
            return size;
        }
    }

    public virtual bool Turbo
    {
        get
        {
            return turbo;
        }
    }

    public virtual void AcceptEngineVisitor(IEngineVisitor visitor)
    {
        // Visit each component first...
        camshaft.AcceptEngineVisitor(visitor);
        piston.AcceptEngineVisitor(visitor);
        foreach (SparkPlug eachSparkPlug in sparkPlugs)
        {
            eachSparkPlug.AcceptEngineVisitor(visitor);
        }

        // Now visit the receiver...
        visitor.Visit(this);
    }

    public override string ToString()
    {
        return this.GetType().Name + " (" + size + ")";
    }
}
```

Now we shall create an actual implementation of IEngineVisitor so you can see how we can easily add additional functionality to engines without any further changes to any engine hierarchy class. The first thing we shall do is to define some clever electronic gizmo that can be attached to an engine that will automatically check each component and diagnose any faults. We therefore define the EngineDiagnostics class:

```
public class EngineDiagnostics : IEngineVisitor
{
    public virtual void Visit(Camshaft camshaft)
    {
        Console.WriteLine("Diagnosing the camshaft");
    }

    public virtual void Visit(IEngine engine)
    {
        Console.WriteLine("Diagnosing the engine");
    }

    public virtual void Visit(Piston piston)
    {
        Console.WriteLine("Diagnosing the piston");
    }

    public virtual void Visit(SparkPlug sparkPlug)
    {
        Console.WriteLine("Diagnosing a single spark plug");
    }
}
```

We also want to print an inventory of how many of each type of component there is within an engine, so we also have an EngineInventory class:

```
public class EngineInventory : IEngineVisitor
{
    private int camshaftCount;
    private int pistonCount;
    private int sparkPlugCount;

    public EngineInventory()
    {
        camshaftCount = 0;
        pistonCount = 0;
        sparkPlugCount = 0;
    }

    public virtual void Visit(Camshaft camshaft)
    {
        camshaftCount++;
    }

    public virtual void Visit(IEngine engine)
    {
        Console.WriteLine("The engine has: " +
                          camshaftCount +" camshaft(s), " +
                          pistonCount + " piston(s), and " +
                          sparkPlugCount + " spark plug(s)");
    }

    public virtual void Visit(Piston piston)
    {
```

```
        pistonCount++;
    }

    public virtual void Visit(SparkPlug sparkPlug)
    {
        sparkPlugCount++;
    }
}
```

The following diagram summarises how all of these classes interact:

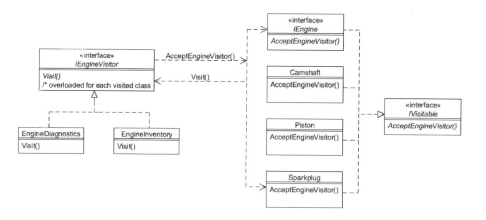

Figure 24.2 : Visitor pattern

Client programs now only need to invoke the AcceptEngineVisitor() method on an instance of IEngine, passing in the appropriate IEngineVisitor object:

```
// Create an engine...
IEngine engine = new StandardEngine(1300);

// Run diagnostics on the engine...
engine.AcceptEngineVisitor(new EngineDiagnostics());
```

The above will result in the following output:

```
Diagnosing the camshaft
Diagnosing the piston
Diagnosing a single spark plug
Diagnosing a single spark plug
Diagnosing a single spark plug
Diagnosing a single spark plug
Diagnosing the unit engine
```

And to obtain the inventory (using the same IEngine instance):

```
// Run inventory on the engine...
engine.AcceptEngineVisitor(new EngineInventory());
```

The output should show:

```
The engine has: 1 camshaft(s), 1 piston(s), and 4 spark plug(s)
```

Part V. Other Useful Patterns

This part describes four additional patterns you should find useful in practical applications.

- *Null Object*: Define a class that enables the processing of `null` values;

- *Simple Factory*: Delegate the instantiation of objects;

- *Model View Controller*: Separate a user interface component's screen representation from its underlying data and functionality;

- *Layers*: Partition an application into separate modular levels that communicate hierarchically.

25. Null Object

As any C# programmer soon discovers, software testing often throws up `NullReferenceException` messages. Sometimes, the only way around this is to specifically test for `null` before performing an operation, which puts an extra onus on the programmer.

Suppose a vehicle's instrument panel contains three slots for warning lights (such as for low oil level or low brake fluid level). A particular vehicle might only use these two lights, with the third slot empty, represented by `null` within C#. Looping through the slots would require a specific test to prevent a `NullReferenceException` being thrown:

```
// OilLevelLight & BrakeFluidLight are each types of IWarningLight
IWarningLight[] lights = new IWarningLight[3];
lights[0] = new OilLevelLight();
lights[1] = new BrakeFluidLight();
lights[2] = null; // empty slot

foreach (IWarningLight currentLight in lights)
{
    If (currentLight != null)
    {
        currentLight.TurnOn();
        currentLight.TurnOff();
        Console.WriteLine(currentLight.On);
    }
}
Console.Read();
```

An approach that can help prevent the need to test for `null` is to create a 'null object' class as part of the class hierarchy. This class will implement the same interface but perform no actual function, as illustrated in the following figure:

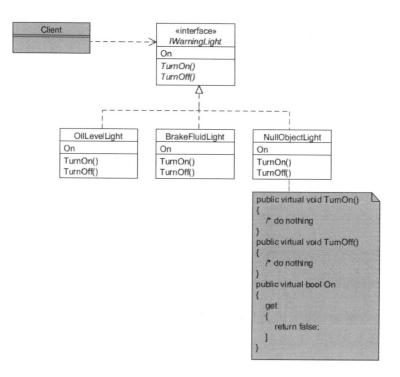

Figure 25.1 : Null Object pattern

The `IWarningLight` interface defines the methods `TurnOn()` and `TurnOff()` and a property getter for `On`:

```
public interface IWarningLight
{
    void TurnOn();
    void TurnOff();
    bool On { get; }
}
```

The `OilLightLevel` and `BrakeFluidLevel` classes each implement the `WarningLight` interface and provide the appropriate code to switch the light on or off:

```
public class OilLevelLight : IWarningLight
{
    private bool on;
```

```
    public virtual void TurnOn()
    {
        on = true;
        Console.WriteLine("Oil level light ON");
    }

    public virtual void TurnOff()
    {
        on = false;
        Console.WriteLine("Oil level light OFF");
    }

    public virtual bool On
    {
        get
        {
            return on;
        }
    }
}


public class BrakeFluidLight : IWarningLight
{
    private bool on;

    public virtual void TurnOn()
    {
        on = true;
        Console.WriteLine("Brake fluid light ON");
    }

    public virtual void TurnOff()
    {
        on = false;
        Console.WriteLine("Brake fluid light OFF");
    }

    public virtual bool On
    {
        get
        {
            return on;
        }
    }
}
```

For the *Null Object* pattern we also create a `NullObjectLight` class that implements the `IWarningLight` interface but performs no actual processing:

```
public class NullObjectLight : IWarningLight
```

```
{
    public virtual void TurnOn()
    {
        // Do nothing...
    }

    public virtual void TurnOff()
    {
        // Do nothing...
    }

    public virtual bool On
    {
        get
        {
            return false;
        }
    }
}
```

Now our client code can be simplified since we no longer need to test if a slot is `null`, provided we make use of the null object:

```
IWarningLight[] lights = new IWarningLight[3];
lights[0] = new OilLevelLight();
lights[1] = new BrakeFluidLight();
lights[2] = new NullObjectLight(); // empty slot

// No need to test for null...
foreach (IWarningLight currentLight in lights)
{
    currentLight.TurnOn();
    currentLight.TurnOff();
    Console.WriteLine(currentLight.On);
}
Console.Read();
```

Note that for *Null Object* getter methods you will need to return whatever seems sensible as a default; hence above the `On` property getter returns `false` since it represents a non-existent light.

26. Simple Factory

In the main section of this book we looked at both the *Factory Method* pattern and the *Abstract Factory* pattern. The *Simple Factory* pattern[1] is a commonly used simplified means of delegating the instantiation of objects to a specific class (the 'factory').

We shall assume here that the Foobar Motor Company manufactures two types of gearbox; an automatic gearbox and a manual gearbox. Client programs might need to create one or the other based upon a condition, as illustrated by the following code fragment (assuming the classes are defined within a class hierarchy):

```
Gearbox selectedGearbox;
if (typeWanted.Equals("automatic"))
{
    selectedGearbox = new AutomaticGearbox();
}
else if (typeWanted.Equals("manual"))
{
    selectedGearbox = new ManualGearbox();
}
// Do something with selectedGearbox...
```

While the above code will of course work, what happens if more than one client program needs to perform a similar selection? We would have to repeat the `if...else...` statements in each client program, and if a new type of gearbox is subsequently manufactured we would have to track down every place the `if...else...` block is used.

Remembering the principle of encapsulating the concept that varies, we can instead delegate the selection and instantiation process to a specific class, known as the 'factory', just for that purpose. Client programs then

---

[1]Some authors state that *Simple Factory* is more of an object-oriented programming idiom rather than a full-fledged pattern.

only make use of the `Create()` method of the factory, as illustrated in the diagram below:

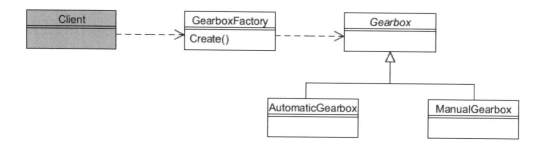

Figure 26.1 : Simple Factory pattern

The abstract `Gearbox` class in our simple example merely defines a no-argument constructor:

```
public abstract class Gearbox
{
    public Gearbox()
    {
    }
}
```

The `AutomaticGearbox` and `ManualGearbox` classes each extend `Gearbox` for their respective types:

```
public class AutomaticGearbox : Gearbox
{
    public AutomaticGearbox()
    {
        Console.WriteLine("New automatic gearbox created");
    }
}
```

```
public class ManualGearbox : Gearbox
{
    public ManualGearbox()
    {
        Console.WriteLine("New manual gearbox created");
    }
}
```

```
}
```

We now need to create our `GearboxFactory` class that is capable of instantiating the appropriate `Gearbox`:

```
public class GearboxFactory
{
    public enum Type
    {
        Automatic, Manual
    }

    public static Gearbox Create(Type type)
    {
        if (type == Type.Automatic)
        {
            return new AutomaticGearbox();
        }
        else
        {
            return new ManualGearbox();
        }
    }
}
```

The `Create()` method takes care of the selection and instantiation, and thus isolates each client program from repeating code. We have made the method `static` purely for convenience; it is not a requirement of the pattern.

Client programs now obtain the type of gearbox by means of the factory:

```
// Create an automatic gearbox
Gearbox auto = GearboxFactory.Create(GearboxFactory.Type.Automatic);

// Create a manual gearbox
Gearbox manual = GearboxFactory.Create(GearboxFactory.Type.Manual);
```

27. Model View Controller

The Foobar Motor Company's satellite-navigation system includes a visual display of the current location, the direction of travel and an indication of the current speed. There is also an input device; controls where you set the destination, etc. A fully fledged simulation is far beyond the scope of this book, so instead we will use a very simplified interface that merely lets you set the direction of travel (North, South, West and East) and the current speed, without regard to any roads, etc..

The user interface will look like this:

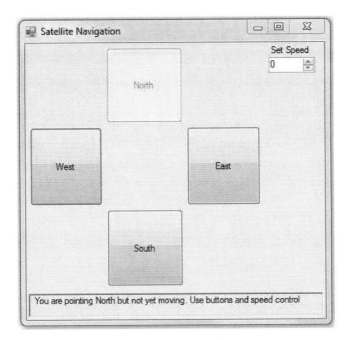

Figure 27.1 : Satellite navigation user interface

As you can see from the above, there are buttons to change direction and a combo-box to adjust the speed. The 'Feedback' section at the bottom of the screen automatically adjusts itself to your selections. Note that each time you click one of the direction buttons that button is disabled, and the previously selected button is re-enabled. The program initially starts by pointing North but with a speed of zero.

This is a straightforward program that would be entirely possible to code within a single class. But as graphical applications become more complex, it greatly simplifies development and maintenance if you separate the major parts of the program.

The *Model View Controller* pattern (often abbreviated to MVC) is a way of achieving a looser coupling between the constituent parts, and is a tried-and-tested approach to graphical applications. There are typically three parts at play in GUI applications:

1. *The "Model"*. This is the 'data' (i.e. state) and associated application or 'business' logic. In our example, this comprises the values of the current direction of travel and the current speed together with methods to update and return them.

2. *The "View"*. This is the graphical display, as shown in Figure 27.1, automatically updating itself as necessary whenever the *Model* changes its state in some way.

3. *The "Controller"*. This is the part that responds to all user input (button clicks, controlling the spinner, etc.) and liaises with both the *Model* and the *View*.

Each of the above three parts will be in a separate class, which can be visualised as follows:

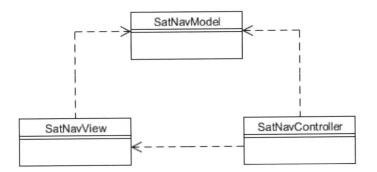

Figure 27.2 : Model View Controller pattern

These classes interrelate in the following way:

•   SatNavModel contains methods to set and get both the direction and speed. It is 'observable'[1] and will notify interested observers whenever either the direction or the speed has changed, but has no direct knowledge of any other class;

•   SatNavView defines the graphical form and user-interface display. It holds a reference to SatNavModel so it can listen to state changes in the *Model* and query its state as needed to keep the display up-to-date automatically;

•   SatNavController holds a reference to both SatNavModel and SatNavView. It handles button clicks and movement of the speed spinner, updating the *Model* and liaising with the *View* as needed.

Just as with the other patterns described in this book, there are variations in how MVC can be structured, and the above might be described as the 'classical' approach. C# typically uses a modified version of MVC in which

---

[1]See the *Observer* pattern

the *View* and *Controller* are combined into a single class, but for the purposes of this book we will use the full three-class separation to present the pattern.

We shall start with the *Model*, which in our case is the class `SatNavModel`. This is coded to have no direct knowledge of either the *View* or the *Controller*, and could therefore be plugged into all sorts of other applications without any changes being required.

```csharp
public class SatNavModel
{
    // The directions we can travel
    public enum TravelDirection
    {
        Still, North, South, East, West
    }

    // Change handler
    public event EventHandler ModelChanged;

    // The current direction and speed
    private TravelDirection CurrentDirection;
    private int CurrentSpeed;

    public SatNavModel()
    {
        CurrentDirection = TravelDirection.North;
        CurrentSpeed = 0;
    }

    public virtual TravelDirection Direction
    {
        set
        {
            if (value != CurrentDirection)
            {
                CurrentDirection = value;
                if (ModelChanged != null)
                {
                    ModelChanged(this, EventArgs.Empty);
                }
            }
        }
        get
        {
            return CurrentDirection;
        }
    }

    public virtual int Speed
```

```
    {
        set
        {
            if (value != CurrentSpeed)
            {
                CurrentSpeed = value;
                if (ModelChanged != null)
                {
                    ModelChanged(this, EventArgs.Empty);
                }
            }
        }
        get
        {
            return CurrentSpeed;
        }
    }
}
```

As you can see, the only link with other classes is through its observers (we are using an `EventHandler` event object to facilitate this). Each time the direction or speed is modified its observers (also known as listeners) are notified.

The graphical display is performed by the `SatNavView` class using standard components. It takes a reference to the `SatNavModel` in its constructor, to register itself as an observer of the model. Whenever it detects a model change the `HandleModelChanged()` method is called, enabling the *View* to update its display accordingly. There are also methods to allow the UI controls to be observed (by, for example, the *Controller*).

```
public partial class SatNavView : Form
{
    private SatNavModel model;
    public event EventHandler ViewControlActivated;

    public SatNavView(SatNavModel model)
    {
        InitializeComponent();
        this.model = model;
        this.model.ModelChanged += HandleModelChanged;
    }

    private void SatNavView_Load(object sender, EventArgs e)
    {
```

```
        northButton.Enabled = false;
        feedbackLabel.Text = "You are pointing " + model.Direction +
            " but not yet moving. Use buttons and speed control";
    }

    public void HandleModelChanged(Object sender, EventArgs args)
    {
        feedbackLabel.Text = "Direction: " + model.Direction +
                             ", speed: " + model.Speed;
    }

    private void eastButton_Click(object sender, EventArgs e)
    {
        if (ViewControlActivated != null)
        {
            ControlEventArgs args = new ControlEventArgs();
            args.direction = SatNavModel.TravelDirection.East;
            ViewControlActivated(this, args);
        }
    }

    private void northButton_Click(object sender, EventArgs e)
    {
        if (ViewControlActivated != null)
        {
            ControlEventArgs args = new ControlEventArgs();
            args.direction = SatNavModel.TravelDirection.North;
            ViewControlActivated(this, args);
        }
    }

    private void southButton_Click(object sender, EventArgs e)
    {
        if (ViewControlActivated != null)
        {
            ControlEventArgs args = new ControlEventArgs();
            args.direction = SatNavModel.TravelDirection.South;
            ViewControlActivated(this, args);
        }
    }

    private void westButton_Click(object sender, EventArgs e)
    {
        if (ViewControlActivated != null)
        {
            ControlEventArgs args = new ControlEventArgs();
            args.direction = SatNavModel.TravelDirection.West;
            ViewControlActivated(this, args);
        }
    }

    private void speedControl_ValueChanged(object sender,
                                           EventArgs e)
    {
        if (ViewControlActivated != null)
        {
            ControlEventArgs args = new ControlEventArgs();
```

```
            args.speed = (int)speedControl.Value;
            ViewControlActivated(this, args);
        }
    }

    internal void enableAllowedButtons()
    {
        // Enable all direction buttons
        eastButton.Enabled = true;
        northButton.Enabled = true;
        southButton.Enabled = true;
        westButton.Enabled = true;

        // Disable current direction button
        if (model.Direction == SatNavModel.TravelDirection.East)
        {
            eastButton.Enabled = false;
        }
        else if (model.Direction == SatNavModel.TravelDirection.North)
        {
            northButton.Enabled = false;
        }
        else if (model.Direction == SatNavModel.TravelDirection.South)
        {
            southButton.Enabled = false;
        }
        else if (model.Direction == SatNavModel.TravelDirection.West)
        {
            westButton.Enabled = false;
        }
    }


    // Nested class for change of direction or speed
    public class ControlEventArgs : EventArgs
    {
        public SatNavModel.TravelDirection direction;
        public int speed;
    }

}
```

The SatNavController class is responsible for handling the user input, which in this case can be either clicking one of the direction buttons or moving the speed spinner. In response to the user input the *Model* state needs to be updated, and there is therefore a reference to both SatNavView and SatNavModel in the constructor. The class sets itself up to listen out for user input and reacts accordingly:

```
public class SatNavController
{
```

```
    // Need a reference to both the model and the view
    private SatNavModel model;
    private SatNavView view;

    public SatNavController(SatNavModel model, SatNavView view)
    {
        this.model = model;
        this.view = view;
        this.view.ViewControlActivated += HandleViewControlActivated;
    }

    public void HandleViewControlActivated(Object sender,
                                              EventArgs args)
    {
        SatNavView.ControlEventArgs satnavArgs
                    = (SatNavView.ControlEventArgs)args;
        if (satnavArgs.direction
                    != SatNavModel.TravelDirection.Still)
        {
            model.Direction = satnavArgs.direction;
            view.enableAllowedButtons();
        }
        else
        {
            model.Speed = satnavArgs.speed;
        }
    }
}
```

Running the application is now as simple as instantiating the above classes from Program.cs:

```
// Create the MVC classes
SatNavModel model = new SatNavModel();
SatNavView view = new SatNavView(model);
SatNavController controller = new SatNavController(model, view);
Application.Run(view);
```

28. Layers

As applications grow larger they can become unwieldy to manage, with lots of interconnections leading to increased coupling. The *Layers* pattern addresses this by partitioning an application into two or more layers in a hierarchy, where each layer communicates only with the layer immediately below it. This approach helps to modularise applications and can help lower the coupling between classes.

Client-server (2-tier) architecture

A simple example of the *Layers* pattern would be the client-server model, where a "client" (such as a web browser) communicates with a "server" (such as a web server) in order to view a web page:

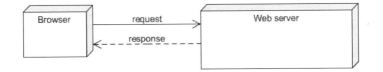

Figure 28.1 Client-server architecture

In Figure 28.1 you can see a browser sending a request to a web server which returns a response (such as a web page). If you imagine the client and server each being in their own namespace, then another way of viewing the above would be as follows:

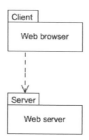

Figure 28.2 : Client-server namespace link

From Figure 28.2 you can infer that an object in the `Client` namespace holds a reference to an object in the `Server` namespace, such that the client can invoke a method on the server which may return a value in response.

> The client-server architecture is also known as a 2-tier architecture. The terms layer and tier are often used interchangeably, but "layer" more accurately refers to a logical partitioning and "tier" to a physical partitioning when each tier is potentially located on a different piece of hardware.

3-tier architecture

A common extension of the client-server architecture is where access to a data store is required, and therefore a third layer (or tier) is added to make a 3-tier architecture:

Figure 28.3 : 3-tier architecture

Figure 28.3 shows the browser sending a request to a server, and the server in turn sending a request to a database to obtain the requested information. This is then returned to the server which in turn returns it to the browser. Viewing the above as separate namespaces gives the following structure:

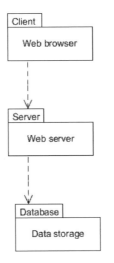

Figure 28.4 : 3-tier namespace links

From figure 28.4 you can infer that an object in the `Client` namespace holds a reference to an object in the `Server` namespace, just as in the 2-tier model. In addition, an object in the `Server` namespace holds a reference to an object in the `Database` namespace. However, the client has no direct access to the database – it has to communicate via the server layer in the middle.

> You are not limited to 3 tiers, of course. As applications grow in complexity additional layers may help to partition systems even further. This leads to the term *n-tier*, where *n* is the number of tiers.

Although the examples above have shown the common usages that typically utilise separate hardware, there is no reason why you cannot apply the structure of the *Layers* pattern in your own self-contained applications. Another pattern you have already seen which can usefully be used in conjunction with *Layers* is the *Façade* pattern, where each layer defines a facade object that the layer above communicates with. This approach can help hide the complexity of each layer behind the façade.

The next chapter provides a worked example that makes use of the *Layers* and *Façade* patterns, along with several other patterns that are commonly found in applications.

Part VI. Design Patterns in Practice

This part consists of a single chapter which shows a small, cut-down application that demonstrates example uses of certain common design patterns as described in this book. The patterns illustrated are:

- *Layers*

- *Singleton*

- *Façade*

- *Factory*

- *Observer*

- *Strategy*

29. Sample 3-Tier Application

This chapter develops a small, sample 3-tier[1] graphical application that makes use of a selection of commonly used design patterns. The application displays a list of engines that have come off the Foobar Motor Company production line (this means that the list may show the same engine type and size more than once), and provides facilities to add new engines and to save & restore the data to persistent storage. Please note that this is not intended to be production level software – the code has been greatly simplified in order to concentrate on the patterns involved.

The finished application will look as follows:

Figure 29.1 : Manage Engines form

Each time the **Build Engine** button is clicked a dialogue will appear enabling you to create a new engine of your chosen type and size to be added to the list:

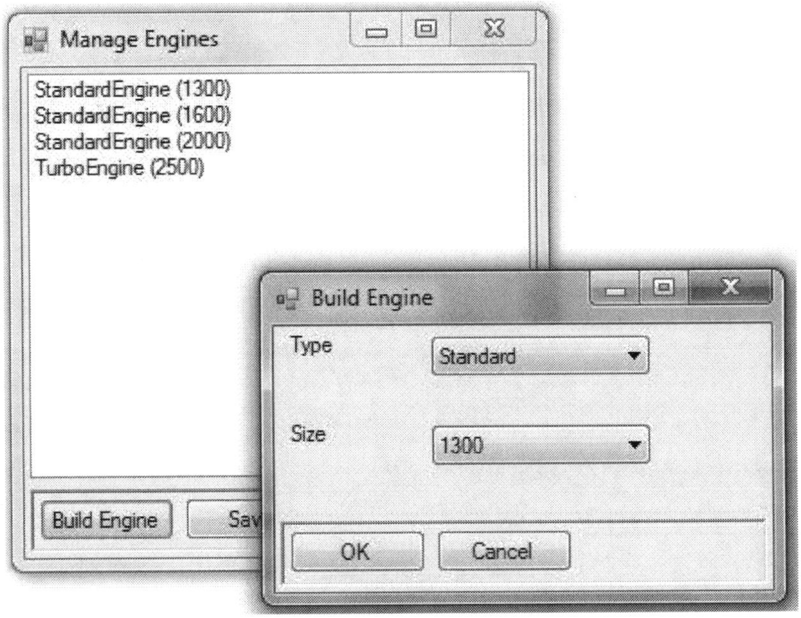

Figure 29.2 : Build Engine form

The **Save** button will store the listed data to a file on your disk and the **Restore** button will replace the listed data with the values of the most recent save.

The application will be designed using a 3-tier architecture using the *Layers* pattern comprising a user interface layer, a business model layer, and a database layer. The classes for each layer will be stored in the namespaces `Business` and `Database` together with the root namespace for the user interface classes. Each layer communicates only with the layer one level below it, as shown in the following figure:

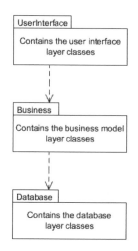

Figure 29.3 : 3-tier Layers pattern as namespaces

The database tier

Starting with the `Database` namespace, we will refer to an object as an `Entity`. Since it is common for database tables to have a primary key we will define the class `EntityKeyGenerator` using the *Singleton* pattern:

```
namespace Database
{
    [Serializable]
    class EntityKeyGenerator
    {
        // static members
        private static volatile EntityKeyGenerator instance;

        public static EntityKeyGenerator Instance
        {
            get
            {
                if (instance == null)
                {
                    instance = new EntityKeyGenerator();
                }
                return instance;
            }
        }
```

```
        }

        // instance variables
        private int nextKey;

        // private constructor
        private EntityKeyGenerator()
        {
        }

        // instance methods
        public virtual int NextKey
        {
            get
            {
                return ++nextKey;
            }
        }
    }
}
```

To generate the next unique key for any `IEngine` entity just needs a call to:

```
EntityKeyGenerator.Instance.NextKey;
```

We will now define a simple `EntityTable` class that can store a dictionary of objects keyed by a sequential numeric id:

```
namespace Database
{
    [Serializable]
    public class EntityTable
    {
        private EntityKeyGenerator keyGenerator;
        private IDictionary<int?, object> entities;
        [field:NonSerialized] public event
                    EventHandler EntityTableItemAdded;
        [field: NonSerialized] public event
                    EventHandler EntityTableRestored;

        internal EntityTable(EntityKeyGenerator keyGenerator)
        {
            this.keyGenerator = keyGenerator;
            entities = new Dictionary<int?, object>();
        }

        internal virtual object GetByKey(int? key)
        {
```

```
            return entities[key];
        }

        internal virtual ICollection<object> All
        {
            get
            {
                return entities.Values;
            }
        }

        internal virtual int? AddEntity(object value)
        {
            int? key = keyGenerator.NextKey;
            entities[key] = value;

            EntityAddedEventArgs args = new EntityAddedEventArgs();
            args.objectAdded = value;
            if (EntityTableItemAdded != null)
            {
                EntityTableItemAdded(this, args);
            }
            return key;
        }

        internal virtual void Restore(EntityTable restoredTable)
        {
            entities.Clear();
            foreach (KeyValuePair<int?, object> pair in
                            restoredTable.entities)
            {
                entities.Add(pair.Key, pair.Value);
            }

            if (EntityTableRestored != null)
            {
                EntityTableRestored(this, EventArgs.Empty);
            }
        }

        // Nested class for entity added eventargs
        public class EntityAddedEventArgs : EventArgs
        {
            public object objectAdded;
        }

    }
}
```

Note the following:

- The constructor requires an `EntityKeyGenerator` object which it can use to generate the next key for this particular entity type;

- The entities are stored in a dictionary keyed by an integer (to represent the primary key) and where the value will be an `object`. This allows the class to store any object type and therefore promotes loose-coupling;

- Methods are provided to return all entities or just one if the key is provided;

- The `AddEntity()` method generates the next primary key which it returns, after adding the entity to the dictionary;

- The `Restore()` method replaces the data with that provided in the argument;

Saving the data to disk will be accomplished either by object serialization or by creating a CSV formatted text file. This suggests the *Strategy* pattern so that either approach can easily be switched in. The `AbstractEntityPersistenceStrategy` class provides the base class to define this:

```
namespace Database
{
    abstract class AbstractEntityPersistenceStrategy
    {
        internal virtual string GetFileName(EntityTable table)
        {
            return table.GetType().Name;
        }

        internal abstract string FileSuffix { get; }
        internal abstract void Save(EntityTable table);
        internal abstract EntityTable Restore(EntityTable table);
    }
}
```

The `EntitySerializationStrategy` class extends the above to implement the required methods:

```
namespace Database
{
    class EntitySerializationStrategy :
            AbstractEntityPersistenceStrategy
```

```
        {
            internal override string FileSuffix
            {
                get
                {
                    return ".ser";
                }
            }

            internal override void Save(EntityTable table)
            {
                Stream stream = File.Open(GetFileName(table) +
                            FileSuffix, FileMode.Create);
                BinaryFormatter formatter = new BinaryFormatter();
                formatter.Serialize(stream, table);
                stream.Close();
            }

            internal override EntityTable Restore(EntityTable table)
            {
                Stream stream = File.Open(GetFileName(table) +
                            FileSuffix, FileMode.Open);
                BinaryFormatter formatter = new BinaryFormatter();
                EntityTable restoredTable =
                    (EntityTable)formatter.Deserialize(stream);
                stream.Close();
                return restoredTable;
            }
        }
    }
}
```

The `EntityCSVStrategy` class likewise could be coded to use a CSV formatted file, although the code is omitted here:

```
namespace Database
{
    class EntityCSVStrategy : AbstractEntityPersistenceStrategy
    {
        internal override string FileSuffix
        {
            get
            {
                return ".csv";
            }
        }

        internal override void Save(EntityTable table)
        {
            // code to save table data in CSV format (omitted)
        }

        internal override EntityTable Restore(EntityTable table)
        {
            // code to restore table data from CSV format (omitted)
```

```
            return table;
        }
    }
}
```

In order to simplify the job of any layer that needs to make use of the database (which will be the `Business` namespace in our case) there will be only a single point of access to all database functionality. This will provide a high-level view of the database which hides the internal structure and so also promotes loose-coupling. The *Façade* pattern used in conjunction with the *Singleton* pattern provides a means of defining a single point of access, as shown in the `DatabaseFacade` class below:

```
namespace Database
{
    [Serializable]
    public class DatabaseFacade
    {
        // static members
        private static volatile DatabaseFacade instance;

        public static DatabaseFacade Instance
        {
            get
            {
                if (instance == null)
                {
                    instance = new DatabaseFacade();
                }
                return instance;
            }
        }

        // instance variables
        private EntityTable engines;
        private AbstractEntityPersistenceStrategy
                        persistenceStrategy;
        public event EventHandler EngineAdded;
        public event EventHandler EnginesRestored;

        // private constructor
        private DatabaseFacade()
        {
            engines = new EntityTable(EntityKeyGenerator.Instance);
            engines.EntityTableItemAdded += HandleEngineAdded;
            engines.EntityTableRestored += HandleEnginesRestored;

            // Set which persistence strategy to use
            // (maybe get from configuration settings somewhere)
            persistenceStrategy = new EntitySerializationStrategy();
        }
```

```
// instance methods

public virtual object[] AllEngines
{
    get
    {
        return engines.All.ToArray();
    }
}

public virtual object GetEngine(int? key)
{
    return engines.GetByKey(key);
}

public virtual int? AddEngine(object engine)
{
    return engines.AddEntity(engine);
}

public virtual void SaveEngines()
{
    persistenceStrategy.Save(engines);
}

public virtual void RestoreEngines()
{
    EntityTable restoredEngines =
            persistenceStrategy.Restore(engines);
    engines.Restore(restoredEngines);
}

public void HandleEngineAdded(Object sender, EventArgs args)
{
    if (EngineAdded != null)
    {
        EngineAdded(sender, args);
    }
}

public void HandleEnginesRestored(Object sender,
                        EventArgs args)
{
    if (EnginesRestored != null)
    {
        EnginesRestored(sender, args);
    }
}

    }
}
```

Note the following:

- The class is a *Singleton*, since the calling layer should only use one *Façade* object;

- The class holds the `EntityTable` object to store the engines and methods to get all or one of them, as well as adding a new engine. If your system also managed vehicles then there would be equivalent variables and methods for this, too;

- The serialization persistence strategy is assumed, but you can see how easy it would be to use alternative strategies;

The layer diagram can now be shown with the classes of the `Database` namespace included:

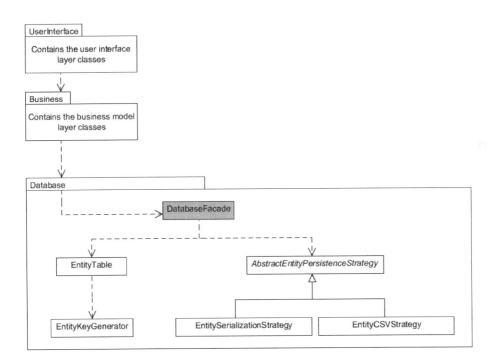

Figure 29.4 : Database layer with Facade class

Note how the `Business` tier communicates only through the `DatabaseFaçade` object. This has the effect of hiding the `Database` layer's complexity behind the façade.

The business tier

Moving on to the `Business` namespace, this will consist primarily of the `IEngine` hierarchy as used throughout this book:

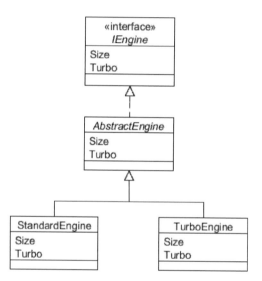

Figure 29.5 : Engine hierarchy

In order to facilitate engine objects being serialised, the class definition of `AbstractEngine` needs to specify that objects are serialisable:

```
namespace Business
{
    [Serializable]
    public abstract class AbstractEngine : IEngine
    {
… Remainder of class omitted …
```

The other classes are unchanged, except that they of course now reside in the namespace called `Business`.

Because there are two types of engine that can exist (standard and turbo), it will be useful to create a *Factory* class that creates objects of the correct type depending upon the supplied arguments. To this end, define a new clas `EngineFactory` in the `Business` layer:

```
namespace Business
{
    class EngineFactory
    {
        public enum Type
        {
            Standard,
            Turbo
        }

        public static IEngine Create(EngineFactory.Type type,
                          int size)
        {
            if (type == Type.Standard)
            {
                return new StandardEngine(size);
            }
            else
            {
                return new TurboEngine(size);
            }
        }

        public static IEngine Create(int size, bool turbo)
        {
            return EngineFactory.Create
                (turbo ? Type.Turbo : Type.Standard, size);
        }

        private EngineFactory()
        {
        }
    }
}
```

Note how the `Create()` method is `static` and is overloaded so that client objects can either supply the enum `Type` value or a `boolean`.

Just as was done for the database layer, the `Business` layer will have its own *façade* object, in this case the `BusinessFacade` singleton:

```
namespace Business
{
    [Serializable]
    public class BusinessFacade
    {
        // static members
        private static volatile BusinessFacade instance;

        public static BusinessFacade Instance
        {
            get
            {
                if (instance == null)
                {
                    instance = new BusinessFacade();
                }
                return instance;
            }
        }


        // instance variables
        public event EventHandler EngineAdded;
        public event EventHandler EnginesRestored;

        // private constructor
        private BusinessFacade()
        {
            DatabaseFacade.Instance.EngineAdded += HandleEngineAdded;
            DatabaseFacade.Instance.EnginesRestored
                    += HandleEnginesRestored;
        }

        // instance methods
        public virtual string[] EngineTypes
        {
            get
            {
                return Enum.GetNames(typeof(EngineFactory.Type));
            }
        }

        public virtual object[] AllEngines
        {
            get
            {
                return DatabaseFacade.Instance.AllEngines;
            }
        }

        public virtual object AddEngine(object type, int size)
        {
            EngineFactory.Type engineType;
```

```
        if (type is string)
        {
            engineType = (EngineFactory.Type)
                    Enum.Parse(typeof(EngineFactory.Type),
                                    (string)type);
        }
        else
        {
            engineType = (EngineFactory.Type)type;
        }
        IEngine engine = EngineFactory.Create
            (size, (engineType == EngineFactory.Type.Turbo));
        DatabaseFacade.Instance.AddEngine(engine);
        return engine;
    }

    public virtual void SaveEngines()
    {
        DatabaseFacade.Instance.SaveEngines();
    }

    public virtual void RestoreEngines()
    {
        DatabaseFacade.Instance.RestoreEngines();
    }

    public void HandleEngineAdded(Object sender, EventArgs args)
    {
        if (EngineAdded != null)
        {
            EngineAdded(sender, args);
        }
    }

    public void HandleEnginesRestored(Object sender,
                            EventArgs args)
    {
        if (EnginesRestored != null)
        {
            EnginesRestored(sender, args);
        }
    }

    }
}
```

Note the following:

- The methods delegate to the appropriate `DatabaseFacade` methods;

- The `AllEngines` getter and `AddEngine()` method return type is `object` rather than `IEngine`. This means that the Business layer will be loosely-coupled with the user interface layer so that the latter does not depend upon the former's implementation details. The user interface can make use of the `ToString()` method of the `object` class to obtain the information to show in its list.

The layer diagram can now be shown with the classes of the `Business` layer included:

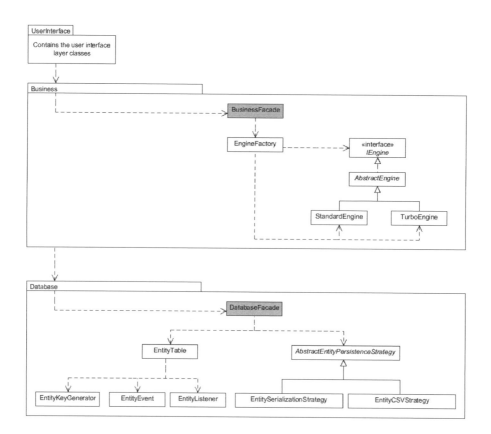

Figure 29.6 : Business layer

Note how the user interface communicates only through the `BusinessFaçade` object. This has the effect of hiding the `Business` layer's complexity behind the façade.

The user interface tier

The user interface layer includes a ManageEngines class which shows a scrollable list of engines and some buttons:

```
public partial class ManageEngines : Form
{
    public ManageEngines()
    {
        InitializeComponent();
        BusinessFacade.Instance.EngineAdded += HandleEngineAdded;
        BusinessFacade.Instance.EnginesRestored
                    += HandleEnginesRestored;
    }

    private void ManageEngines_Load(object sender, EventArgs e)
    {
        // Create some sample data
        BusinessFacade.Instance.AddEngine
                (EngineFactory.Type.Standard, 1300);
        BusinessFacade.Instance.AddEngine
                (EngineFactory.Type.Standard, 1600);
        BusinessFacade.Instance.AddEngine
                (EngineFactory.Type.Standard, 2000);
        BusinessFacade.Instance.AddEngine
                (EngineFactory.Type.Turbo, 2500);
    }

    private void buildEngineButton_Click(object sender,
                        EventArgs e)
    {
        Form buildEngineForm = new BuildEngineForm();
        buildEngineForm.ShowDialog(this);
    }

    public void HandleEngineAdded(Object sender, EventArgs args)
    {
        EntityTable.EntityAddedEventArgs entityArgs =
                (EntityTable.EntityAddedEventArgs)args;
        enginesList.Items.Add(entityArgs.objectAdded.ToString());
    }

    public void HandleEnginesRestored(Object sender,
                        EventArgs args)
    {
        enginesList.Clear();
        foreach (object engine in
                BusinessFacade.Instance.AllEngines)
        {
            enginesList.Items.Add(engine.ToString());
        }
    }
```

```
        private void saveButton_Click(object sender, EventArgs e)
        {
            BusinessFacade.Instance.SaveEngines();
        }

        private void restoreButton_Click(object sender, EventArgs e)
        {
            BusinessFacade.Instance.RestoreEngines();
        }

    }
```

The **Build Engine** button creates and displays a `BuildEngineForm` object, which is as follows:

```
public partial class BuildEngineForm : Form
{
    public BuildEngineForm()
    {
        InitializeComponent();
    }

    private void BuildEngineForm_Load(object sender, EventArgs e)
    {
        // Load engine types combo
        object[] engineTypes = BusinessFacade.Instance.EngineTypes;
        foreach (object obj in engineTypes)
        {
            typeCombo.Items.Add(obj.ToString());
        }
        typeCombo.SelectedIndex = 0;

        // Load engine size combo
        sizeCombo.Items.Add(1300);
        sizeCombo.Items.Add(1600);
        sizeCombo.Items.Add(2000);
        sizeCombo.Items.Add(2500);
        sizeCombo.SelectedIndex = 0;
    }

    private void cancelButton_Click(object sender, EventArgs e)
    {
        this.Close();
    }

    private void okButton_Click(object sender, EventArgs e)
    {
        BusinessFacade.Instance.AddEngine
                (typeCombo.SelectedItem,
                        (int)sizeCombo.SelectedItem);
        this.Close();
    }
}
```

The **OK** button invokes the appropriate `BusinessFacade` method to add an engine with your selected criteria. On the main list panel the **Save** and **Restore** buttons also make appropriate calls to the `BusinessFacade` object methods so that the currently displayed data can be saved or restored.

Part VII. Appendixes

This part contains the appendixes, which includes a brief explanation of the Unified Modeling Language (UML) diagram formats for those unfamiliar with UML, and a quick reference for each of the 23 main patterns.

Appendix A.   UML Diagrams

This book uses a simplified version of Unified Modeling Language (UML) diagrams to illustrate class hierarchies and usages for the patterns in this book. Each separate class is shown as a bounded rectangle with three horizontal sections, the top section containing the name of the class, the second section any relevant state (i.e. properties and instance variables) and the third section containing the protocol (i.e. methods).

Representing types

Abstract classes, interfaces and abstract methods are shown in italicised text. The following figure shows an example of each sort of type and method:

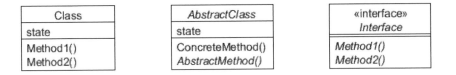

Figure A.1 : Normal class (left), abstract class (centre), interface (right)

In this book any properties and relevant instance variables will be shown in the "state" section. The "method" section will only show relevant methods and not property getters or setters. Unless specified otherwise, you can assume that all listed methods are `public`.

Representing inheritance

Inheritance is shown by a line connection between classes, with a hollow triangle pointing to the class being inherited or interfaces being implemented. Solid lines are shown for classes and dashed lines for interface connections:

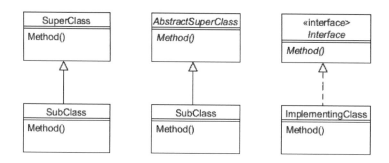

Figure A.2 : Extending a class (left & centre), implementing an interface (right)

Representing composition and usage

When one class 'uses' another (i.e. holds a reference to it), this is shown by a dashed line with an open arrow pointing toward the class being used. The usage is usually through being an instance variable or by passing a reference to an object's constructor or a method, or by instantiating the used object. In the following diagram each instance of ClassA holds or obtains a reference to an instance of ClassB:

Figure A.3 : ClassA uses ClassB

Code snippets

Where useful, snippets of code will be shown in a grey box attached to a class with a dashed line:

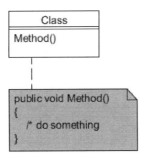

Figure A.4 : Code snippet

'Client' and other grey coloured classes

If a class rectangle is shown in grey this only for aesthetic purposes to separate it from other classes in the diagram. This is most often used in this book for 'client' classes, i.e. classes which make use of a particular pattern, as the following example for the *Chain of Responsibility* pattern illustrates:

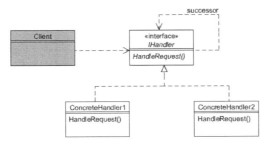

Figure A.5 : Client class in grey

Appendix B. Design Pattern Quick Reference

This appendix provides an alphabetical quick-reference of each of the 23 main design patterns described in this book in their most general form.

Note that many of the patterns make use of abstract classes or interfaces. In most cases these are interchangeable and the choice of which to use depends entirely upon your project requirements. It may also appear that the general form of a particular pattern described in this chapter differs from the detailed example in the main body of this book, but this is just a consequence of the fact that patterns are adaptable to the needs of the situation, and the general form should not be construed as the only or 'correct' approach.

Abstract Factory

Type	Creational
Purpose	Provide an interface for creating families of related or dependent objects without specifying their concrete classes.
Example usage	Commonly used when generating graphical 'widgets' for different look-and-feels.
Consequences	Isolates concrete classes. Enables easy exchange of product families. Promotes consistency among products.

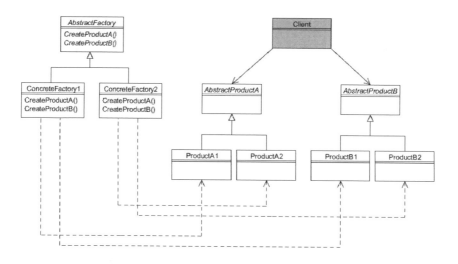

• `AbstractFactory` defines an interface for methods that create abstract product objects;

• `ConcreteFactory1` and `ConcreteFactory2` take care of instantiating the appropriate product families (e.g. `ConcreteFactory1` creates `ProductA1` and `ProductB1`);

• `AbstractProductA` and `AbstractProductB` defines the interface of each different type of product;

Client programs only use the interfaces declared by `AbstractFactory` and `AbstractProductA` and `AbstractProductB`.

Adapter

Type	Structural
Purpose	Convert the interface of a class into another interface clients expect. Adapter lets classes work together that couldn't otherwise because of incompatible interfaces.
Example usage	Integration of independent and incompatible classes.
Consequences	A single adapter can work with many adaptees.

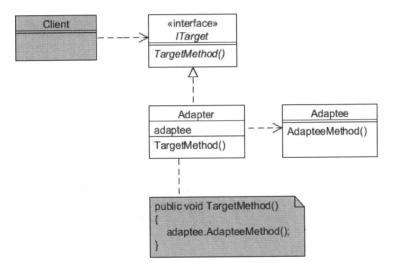

• `ITarget` refers to the interface that the client program requires;

• `Adapter` is the class used by client programs to forward requests to `Adaptee`;

• `Adaptee` is the class that needs adapting.

Bridge

Type	Structural
Purpose	Decouple an abstraction from its implementation so that each may vary independently.
Example usage	GUI frameworks and persistence frameworks.
Consequences	An implementation is not permanently bound to an interface, and can be switched at run-time.

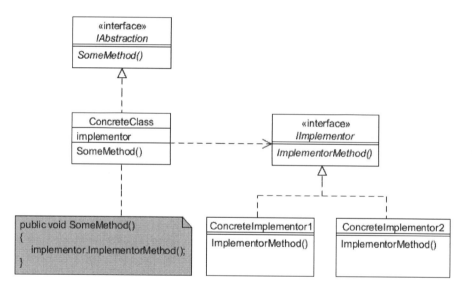

• IAbstraction is the abstraction of the interface;

• ConcreteClass implements the IAbstraction interface and holds a reference to IImplementor. It provides an implementation in terms of IImplementor;

• IImplementor is the implementation interface which may be quite different to the IAbstraction interface;

• ConcreteImplementor1 and ConcreteImplementor2 implement the IImplementor interface.

Builder

Type	Creational
Purpose	Separate the construction of a complex object from its representation so that the same construction process can create different representations.
Example usage	Useful when there are several steps needed to create an object.
Consequences	Enables variations of a products internal representation. Isolates construction and representation.

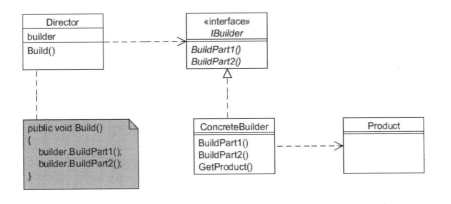

- IBuilder defines an interface for creating parts of a 'product' object;

- ConcreteBuilder creates and assembles the 'product' parts step-by-step and provides a method to retrieve it during or after assembly;

- Director controls the actual assembly process.

Chain of Responsibility

Type	Behavioural
Purpose	Avoid coupling the sender of a request to its receiver by giving more than one object a chance to handle the request. Chain the receiving objects and pass the request along the chain until an object handles it.
Example usage	When more than one object can handle a request and the handler is not known in advance.
Consequences	Not every request needs to be handled, or maybe it needs to be handled by more than one handler.

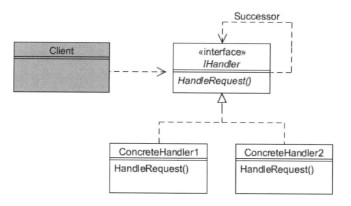

•   `IHandler` defines an interface for handling requests;

•   `ConcreteHandler1` and `ConcreteHandler2` each decide if they can handle the request itself or if it should be passed on to its successor.

Client programs send their requests to the first object in the chain.

Command

Type	Behavioural
Purpose	Encapsulate a request as an object, thereby letting you parameterise clients with different requests, queue or log requests, and support undoable operations.
Example usage	UI controls such as menu items and toolbar buttons. Undo/redo mechanisms.
Consequences	Strive to keep separate the object that invokes the operation from the object that performs it.

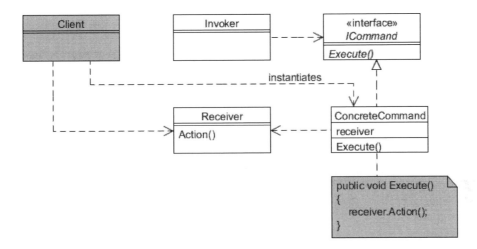

- `ICommand` is the interface for executing an operation;

- `ConcreteCommand` performs the operation on the `Receiver`;

- `Invoker` asks the command to be carried out;

- `Receiver` knows how to perform the operations.

Composite

Type	Structural
Purpose	Compose objects into tree structures to represent part-whole hierarchies. Composite lets clients treat individual objects and compositions of objects uniformly.
Example usage	Graphical component hierarchies, etc.
Consequences	Simple objects can be combined into complex assemblies and all treated through a common interface. Adding new components should be straightforward.

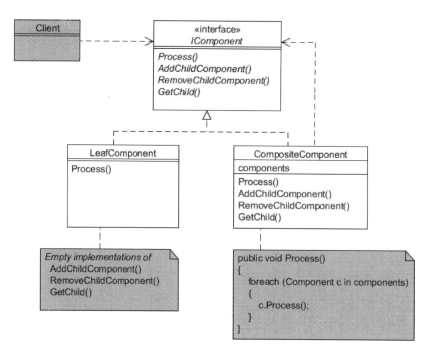

- IComponent is the interface for both leaves and composites;

- LeafComponent defines objects that have no children;

- CompositeComponent defines objects that may have children.

Decorator

Type	Structural
Purpose	Attach additional responsibilities to an object dynamically. Decorators provide a flexible alternative to subclassing for extending functionality.
Example usage	GUI toolkits file and object input/output streams (e.g. buffering).
Consequences	Can be more flexible than direct inheritance and reduce number of classes required.

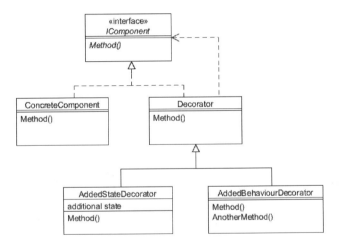

- `IComponent` defines the interface for objects that can have responsibilities added to them dynamically;

- `ConcreteComponent` implements the `IComponent` interface;

- `Decorator` maintains a reference to an `IComponent` object as well as defining an interface that matches that of `IComponent`;

- `AddedStateDecorator` and `AddedBehaviourDecorator` each decorate an `IComponent` by adding additional instance variables and/or methods.

Facade

Type	Structural
Purpose	Provide a unified interface to a set of interfaces in a subsystem. Facade defines a higher-level interface that makes the subsystem easier to use.
Example usage	To simplify access to several objects through a single 'facade' object.
Consequences	Needs a new class to be created to serve as the 'facade'.

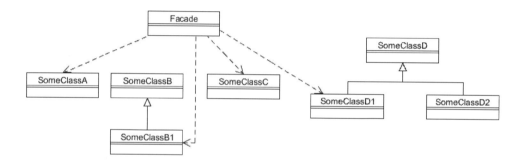

- Facade defines the class that provides the simplified interface to other classes;

- SomeClassA, *etc.* are various classes, related or not.

Factory Method

Type	Creational
Purpose	Define an interface for creating an object, but let subclasses decide which class to instantiate.
Example usage	When you can't anticipate the specific type of object to be created, or you want to localise the knowledge of which class gets created.
Consequences	Reduces the need for clients to use 'new' to instantiate objects.

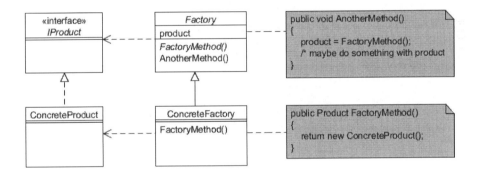

- `IProduct` defines the interface of the product that is to be created;

- `ConcreteProduct` is an implementation of a particular product;

- `Factory` declares the factory method that returns an `IProduct` object;

- `ConcreteFactory` implements the factory method defined in `Factory` to return an instance of `IProduct`.

Flyweight

Type	Structural
Purpose	Use sharing to support large numbers of fine-grained objects efficiently.
Example usage	Text/graphic editors, etc.
Consequences	Saves memory through sharing shared state.

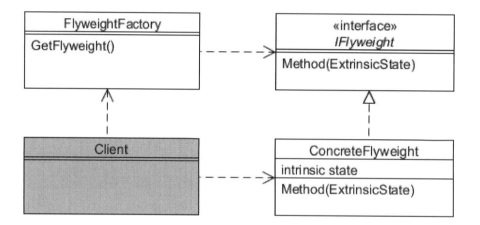

• `IFlyweight` defines the interface through which flyweight objects can act on extrinsic state;

• `ConcreteFlyweight` implements `Flyweight` and stores intrinsic state. Must be shareable;

• `FlyweightFactory` creates and manages the flyweight objects through a 'pooling' mechanism.

Client programs maintain references to the flyweights obtained through the factory.

Interpreter

Type	Behavioural
Purpose	Given a language, define a representation for its grammar along with an interpreter that uses the representation to interpret sentences in the language.
Example usage	Simple grammars and mini-language processing.
Consequences	Not suitable for complex grammars and language processing.

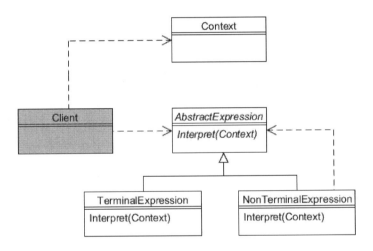

• `AbstractExpression` **defines the abstract method to interpret an element;**

• `TerminalExpression` **extends** `AbstractExpression` **for language elements that terminate an expression;**

• `NonTerminalExpression` **extends** `AbstractExpression` **for language elements that are just part of an expression;**

• `Context` **is the object that is being parsed (e.g. the grammar or language).**

Iterator

Type	Behavioural
Purpose	Provide a way to access the elements of an aggregate object sequentially without exposing its underlying representation.
Example usage	Wherever a collection or array of objects or values need to be processed in turn.
Consequences	The for-each syntax simplifies usage.

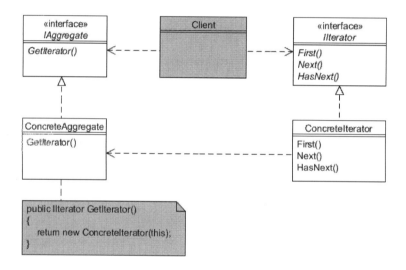

• IIterator defines the interface for the iterator;

• ConcreteIterator implements IIterator to perform the processing of each element in IAggregate;

• IAggregate defines the interface for the collection to be processed;

• ConcreteAggregate implements IAggregate for the actual collection.

Mediator

Type	Behavioural
Purpose	Define an object that encapsulates how a set of objects interact. Mediator promotes loose coupling by keeping objects from referring to each other explicitly, and it lets you vary their interaction independently.
Example usage	Dialogs that control UI components, etc.
Consequences	The Mediator could be defined to use the Observer pattern to monitor the components.

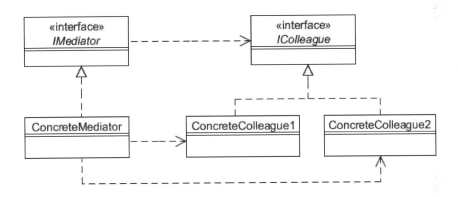

• IMediator defines the interface for communication with IColleague objects;

• ConcreteMediator implements the IMediator interface and performs the communication;

• IColleague defines the interface for a component that needs communication with the IMediator;

• ConcreteColleague1 and ConcreteColleague2 implement the IColleague interface and perform the communication with the IMediator such that it needs no knowledge of any other IColleague.

Memento

Type	Behavioural
Purpose	Without violating encapsulation, capture and externalise an object's internal state so that it can be restored to this state later.
Example usage	Undo & Redo processing, database transactions, etc.
Consequences	Encapsulates the storage of state external to the originating object, but might be expensive in terms of memory or performance.

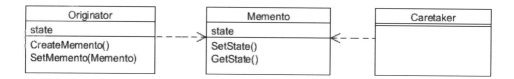

- Originator creates the Memento object and uses it to restore its state;

- Memento stores the state of Originator;

- Caretaker keeps the memento.

Observer

Type	Behavioural
Purpose	Define a one-to-many dependency between objects so that when one object changes its state, all its dependants are notified and updated automatically.
Example usage	GUI controls, events, etc.
Consequences	Decouples classes through a common interface.

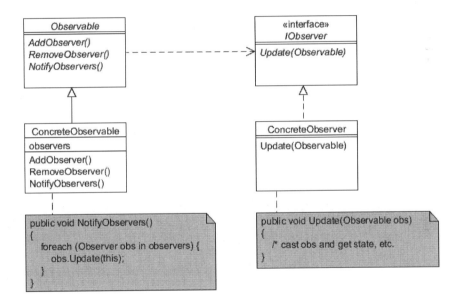

• `Observable` defines the mechanisms to register observers and notify them of events;

• `ConcreteObservable` extends `Observable` for a particular subject class;

• `IObserver` defines an interface for interested classes;

• `ConcreteObserver` implements `IObserver` for a particular interested class.

Prototype

Type	Creational
Purpose	Specify the kinds of objects to create using a prototypical instance, and create new objects by copying the prototype.
Example usage	Where easier or faster to clone than to instantiate.
Consequences	Cloning might become difficult in certain situations

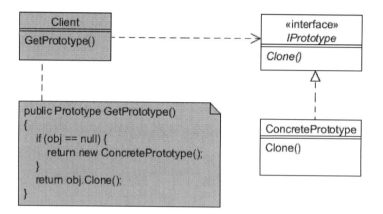

- `IPrototype` defines an interface that can 'clone' itself;

- `ConcretePrototype` performs the self-cloning.

Client programs create new objects by asking a prototype to clone itself.

Proxy

Type	Structural
Purpose	Provide a surrogate or place-holder for another object to control access to it.
Example usage	Network connections, security proxies, etc.
Consequences	Possible decrease in performance.

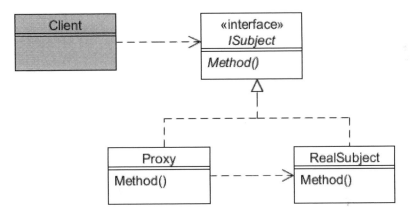

- `ISubject` defines the interface that needs to be accessed through a proxy;

- `RealSubject` defines the actual object which `Proxy` represents;

- `Proxy` maintains a reference to `RealSubject` so it can act on its behalf.

Singleton

Type	Creational
Purpose	Ensure a class allows only one object to be created, providing a single point of access to it.
Example usage	Log files, configuration settings, etc.
Consequences	Often overused, difficult to subclass, can lead to tight coupling.

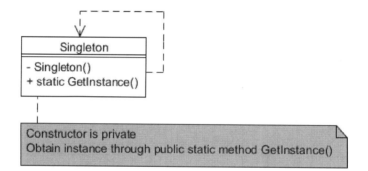

- Singleton defines a `private` constructor together with a `public` class (i.e. `static`) method as the only means of getting the instance.

State

Type	Behavioural
Purpose	Allow an object to alter its behaviour when its internal state changes. The object will appear to change its class.
Example usage	UI shape components, etc.
Consequences	Localises state-specific behaviour and separates behaviour for different states.

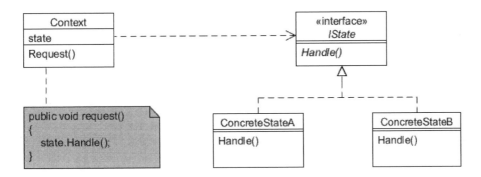

- `IState` defines the interface for handling different states in the `handle()` method;

- `ConcreteStateA` and `ConcreteStateB` implement the `IState` interface for each separate state;

- `Context` holds a reference to an `IState` object to request a particular state.

Strategy

Type	Behavioural
Purpose	Define a family of algorithms, encapsulate each one, and make them interchangeable. Strategy lets the algorithm vary independently from clients that use it.
Example usage	Need to change algorithms
Consequences	Might need to pass data to each strategy.

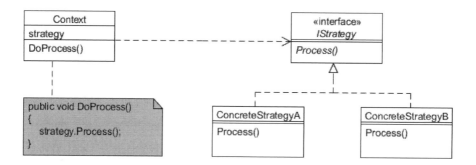

- `IStrategy` **defines the interface for the algorithms;**

- `ConcreteStrategyA` **and** `ConcreteStrategyB` **implement** `IStrategy` **for a particular algorithm;**

- `Context` **holds a reference to the** `IStrategy` **that is being used.**

Template Method

Type	Behavioural
Purpose	Define the skeleton of an algorithm in a method, deferring some steps to subclasses. Template Method lets subclasses redefine certain steps of an algorithm without changing the algorithm's structure.
Example usage	When an algorithm's steps can be performed in different ways.
Consequences	Should prevent the template method from being overridden.

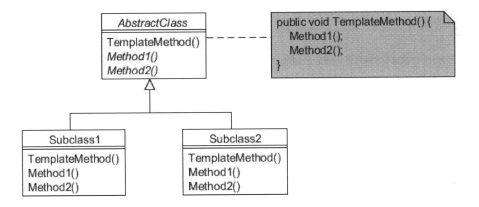

• `AbstractClass` defines the non-overridable `TemplateMethod()` that invokes a series of abstract methods defined in subclasses;

• `Subclass1` and `Subclass2` extend `AbstractClass` to define the code for each abstract method invoked by `TemplateMethod()`.

Visitor

Type	Behavioural
Purpose	Represent a method to be performed on the elements of an object structure. Visitor lets you define a new method without changing the classes of the elements on which it operates.
Example usage	Similar operations need performing on different types in a structure, or as a means to add functionality without extensive modifications.
Consequences	Adding new visitable objects can require modifying visitors.

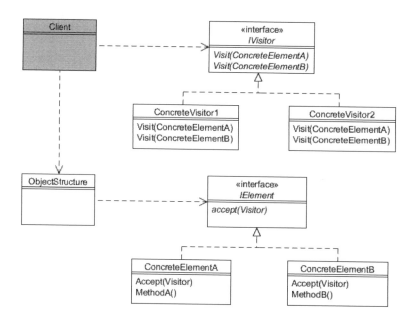

- IVisitor defines the interface that declares methods to visit each kind of visitable IElement;

- ConcreteVisitor1 and ConcreteVisitor2 implement the IVisitor interface for each element that could be visited;

- IElement defines the interface for all classes which could be visited;

- `ConcreteElementA` and `ConcreteElementB` implement the `IElement` interface for each class that could be visited.

- `ObjectStructure` contains references to all objects that can be visited, enabling iteration through them.

Appendix C. Bibliography

Beck, Kent. *Extreme programming explained; Embrace Change.* Reading, MA: Addison-Wesley, 1999.

Bevis, Tony. *Java design pattern essentials - second edition.* Essex, UK. Ability First Limited 2012.

Bevis, Tony. *Java programming step-by-step.* Essex, UK. Ability First Limited 2012.

Bloch, Joshua. *Effective Java: programming language guide.* River, NJ: Addison-Wesley, 2001.

Cooper, James W. *Java design patterns: a tutorial.* Reading, MA: Addison-Wesley, 2000.

Court, Lindsey, et al. *Software development with Java.* Milton Keynes, The Open University, 2007.

Fowler, Martin, et al. *Refactoring: improving the design of existing code.* River, NJ: Addison-Wesley, 2000.

Fowler, Martin, and Kendall Scott. *UML distilled, second edition: a brief guide to the standard object modeling language.* River, NJ: Addison-Wesley, 1999.

Freeman, Eric, et al. *Head first design patterns.* Sebastopol, CA : O'Reilly, 2004.

Gamma, Erich, et al. *Design patterns: elements of reusable object-oriented software.* River, NJ: Addison-Wesley, 1995.

Gilbert, Stephen, and Bill McCarty. *object-oriented design in Java.* Corte Madera, CA: Waite Group Press, 1998.

Laney, Robin, et al. *Software engineering with objects.* Milton Keynes, The Open University, 2008.

Langr, Jeff. *Java Style: patterns for implementation.* River, NJ: Prentice-Hall PTR, 2000.

Index